PHILIP'S *Red Books* showing

LOCAL STREET ATLAS

CW00501181

HIGH WYCOMBE
AMERSHAM

BEACONSFIELD · BOURNE END · GERRARDS CROSS
MARLOW · PRINCES RISBOROUGH · STOKENCHURCH

CONTENTS

	B Road
	Minor Road
	Pedestrianized / Restricted Access
	Track
	Built Up Area
- - - - -	Footpath
	Stream
	River
Lock	Canal
▬	Railway / Station
●	Post Office
P P+▭▭	Car Park / Park & Ride
ⓒ	Public Convenience
✛	Place of Worship
→	One-way Street
i	Tourist Information Centre
▲8 ▲8	Adjoining Pages
	Area Depicting Enlarged Centre
	Emergency Services
	Industrial Buildings
	Leisure Buildings
	Education Buildings
	Hotels etc.
	Retail Buildings
	General Buildings
	Woodland
	Orchard
	Recreational / Parkland
	Cemetery

www.philips-maps.co.uk

First published in 2006 by
Estate Publications

This edition published by Philip's,
a division of Octopus Publishing Group Ltd
www.octopusbooks.co.uk
2–4 Heron Quays, London E14 4JP
An Hachette Livre UK Company

Second impression 2008
08/06-06

ISBN 978-0-540-09360-1

© Philip's 2008

 Ordnance Survey®

This product includes mapping data licensed
from Ordnance Survey®, with the permission
of the Controller of Her Majesty's Stationery
Office.© Crown copyright 2006. All rights
reserved. Licence number 100011710

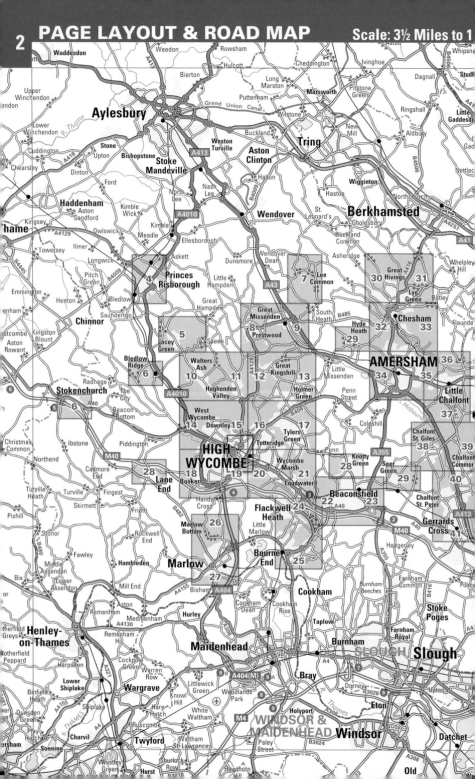

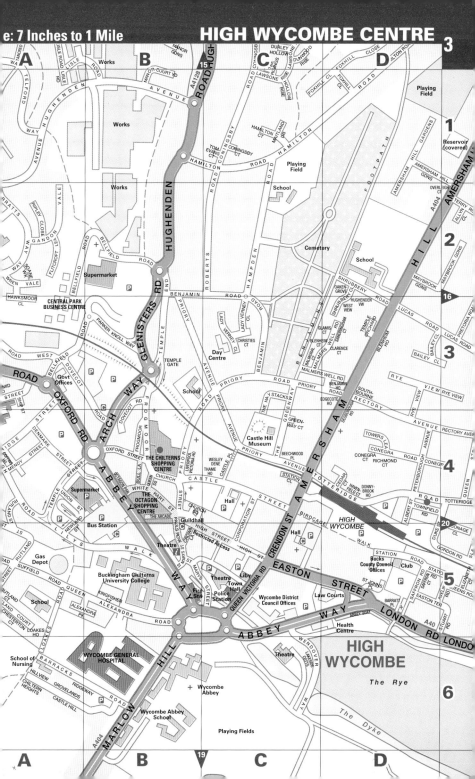

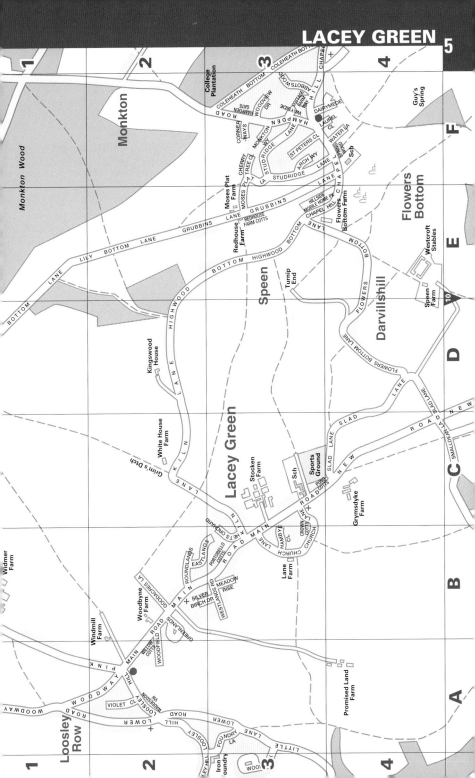

Loosley Row

Monkton Wood

Monkton

College Plantation

COLEHEATH BOTTOM

COLEHEATH BOTTOM

ABBOTS WOOD

CHAPEL

HILL

Guy's Spring

WOODVIEW DR

MONKTON GATE

HAMPDEN LANE

MONKTON WY

CORNER WAYS

WAYSIDE

DAIRYMEDE

LAUREL CL

WATER LA

Sch

CHERRY TREE CL

MOSES PLAT LA

STUDRIDGE LA

St PETERS CL

ARCH WY

SPRING WD

STUDRIDGE

Moses Plat Farm

MOSES

GRUBBINS

LANE

HILLSIDE

MOBILE HOME PK

CHAPEL HILL

Flowers Bottom Farm

CHAPEL LANE

Redhouse Farm

REDHOUSE FARM COTTS

LANE

Flowers Bottom

GRUBBINS LANE

LILY BOTTOM LANE

HIGHWOOD BOTTOM

Speen

Turnip End

Westcroft Stables

BOTTOM

HIGHWOOD

BOTTOM LANE

FLOWERS BOTTOM

Darvillshill

Speen Farm

E

D

Kingswood House

HIGHWOOD LANE

FLOWERS BOTTOM LANE

White House Farm

KILN LANE

Grim's Dtch

Lacey Green

SLAD

SLAD LANE

NEW

ROAD

SMALLDEAN LA

SLAD LANE

Stocken Farm

Sch

Sports Ground

NEW ROAD

SLAD LANE

C

KILN LANE

KEEPS ORCHARD

PORTOBELLO COTTS

ROUNDLANDS

EASTLANDS

MEADOW RISE

MAIN ROAD

HAMBY'F CL

CHURCH LANE

CROWN LANE COTTS

POND

COTTS

Grymsdyke Farm

Widmer Farm

Woodbyne Farm

GOODACRES LA

SILVER BIRCH RD

WESTLANDS RD

Lane Farm

CHURCH LANE

B

Windmill Farm

MAIN ROAD

GREENLANDS

WOODFIELD

WILLOW COTTS

PINK HILL

WOODWAY

WOODWAY

ROAD

LOWER ROAD

LOWER

WIDMERSON VW

VIOLET LA

LOOSLEY HILL

FOUNDRY LA

LITTLE LANE

Iron Foundry

WOO...

A

1

2

3

4

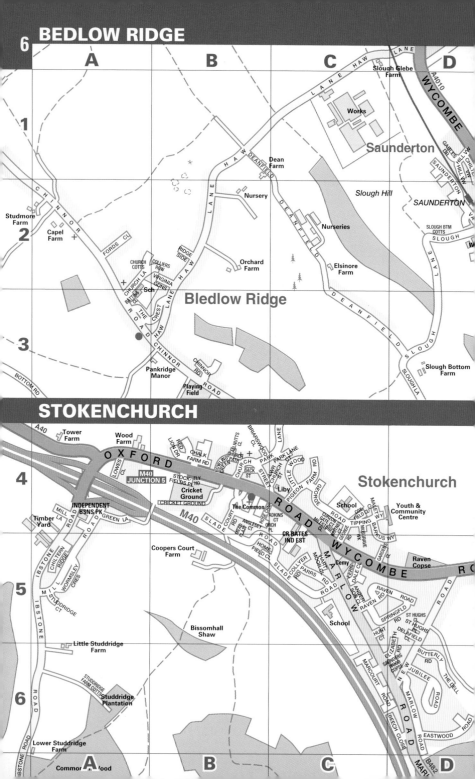

A   **B**   **C**   **D**

LANE HAW LANE

Slough Glebe Farm

WYCOMBE

A4010

Works

Saunderton

GABLES HILL VW CHILT HILL VW

SAUNDERTON DR

LANE

HAW

DEANFIELD

Dean Farm

Slough Hill

SAUNDERTON

CHINNOR

Nursery

DEANFIELD

Studmore Farm

Capel Farm

SAUNDERTON VA

Nurseries

SLOUGH BTM COTTS

SLOUGH

W

2

FORDS CL

COLLIERS ROW

RIDGE SIDE

Orchard Farm

Elsinore Farm

CHURCH COTTS

VIRGINIA GDNS

HAW LANE

DEANFIELD

CHURCH LA

BATING

Sch

THE CREST

Bledlow Ridge

SLOUGH

3

ROAD

HAW

CHINNOR

DEANFIELD

SLOUGH LA

Pankridge Manor

CHINNOR RD

Slough Bottom Farm

BOTTOM RD

ROAD

Playing Field

STOKENCHURCH

A40

Tower Farm

Wood Farm

LANE

PARK LANE

Stokenchurch

WYCOMBE

4

OXFORD

RED LION DR

LOWES CT

M40 JUNCTION 5

CHALK FARM RD

STOCK FIELDS PL

BRIARSWOOD

BUILDINGS CL

CHURCH NUTTS CL

CHURCH ST

BACK ST

PARK STREET

CHWR PARK LANE

LITTLE WOOD

PIGEON FARM RD

GEORGE RD

MAEVY ST

BARN CL

MUSBRANE WK

BUS WY

TIPPING

School

Youth & Community Centre

INDEPENDENT BSNS PK

MILL LA

GREEN LA

Cricket Ground

ELY HO

Liby

The Common

ANGLESEY CT

ADKINS CT

ORCH

CR BATES IND EST

PIGEON CL

GATE RD

MILBURNE WK

GORSE CL

FIELD RD

GARDEN RD

Raven Copse

Timber Yard

CHILTERN RIDGE

WORMSLEY CRES

IBSTONE

Coopers Court Farm

HOME FIELD CL

SLADE COURT

SLADE ROAD

COLYER PL

PARRS

MART RD

MORRIS RD

DALE CL

PEREE RD

Cemy

RAVEN RD

RAVEN ROAD

SPRINGFLD RD

ANSTEY RD

ROAD

MARLOW

ROAD

5

MILL CT

STUDDRIDGE

IBSTONE

Bissomhall Shaw

SLADE

HUNT

ST HUGHS RD

ST HUGHS CL

DELAFIELD CL

School

6

ROAD

Little Studdridge Farm

STUDDRIDGE FARM COTTS

Studdridge Plantation

ELIZABETH RD

MARCOURT RD

SAUNDERS WOOD COPSE

JUBILEE RD

BUTTERLY RD

THE DELL ROAD

MARLOW ROAD

BEECH CLOSE

EASTWOOD

B482

R

Lower Studdridge Farm

ROAD

Common Wood

A   **B**   **C**   **D**

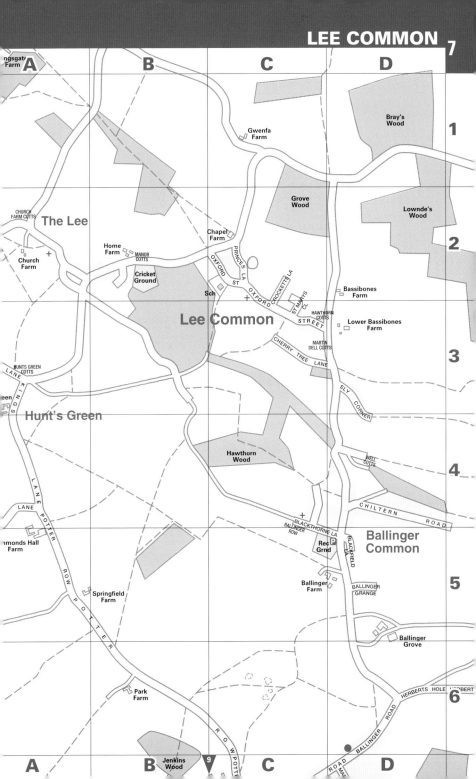

ngsgate Farm
A
B
C
D

1

Bray's Wood

Gwenfa Farm

Grove Wood

Lownde's Wood

CHURCH FARM COTTS

The Lee

2

Chapel Farm

Home Farm

MANOR COTTS

Church Farm

Cricket Ground

PRINCE'S LA

OXFORD ST

OXFORD

CROCKETT'S LA

ST MARYS CL

Bassibones Farm

HAWTHORN COTTS

Sch

STREET

Lower Bassibones Farm

Lee Common

MARTIN DELL COTTS

CHERRY TREE LANE

3

HUNTS GREEN COTTS

LANE KINGS

SLY CORNER

een

Hunt's Green

Hawthorn Wood

WELL COTTS

4

LANE

LANE POTTER

CHILTERN ROAD

mmonds Hall Farm

BLACKTHORNE LA
BALLINGER ROW

Rec Grnd

Ballinger Common

ROW POTTER

BLACKFIELD LA

Springfield Farm

Ballinger Farm

BALLINGER GRANGE

5

Ballinger Grove

6

Park Farm

HERBERTS HOLE

HERBERT

BALLINGER ROAD

ROW POTTER

A
B

Jenkins Wood

9

C

ROAD

D

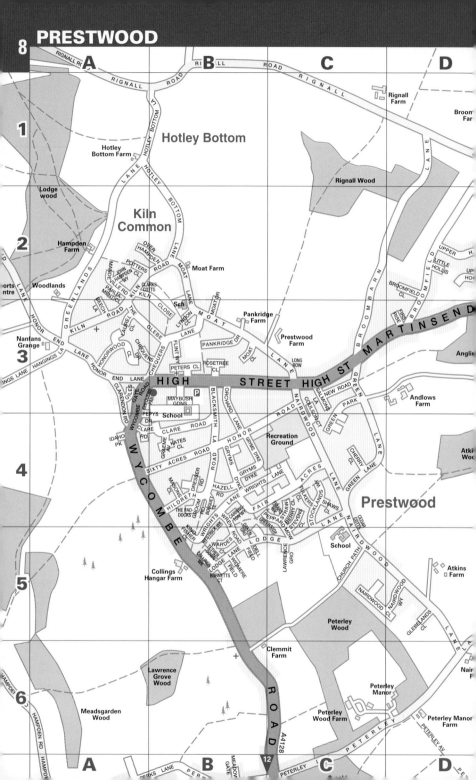

E   **F**   **G**   7   **H**

A413

AYLESBURY

GREAT

Mobwell

Jenkins Wood

Bury Farm

ROW POTTER ROW

KINGS

BAL

1

HEADLAND

ROBSON CL

ROAD

WINSLOW

GARTH

TANTON HO

WINSLOW FIELD

Sch

WATLINGTON CT

ELMHURST

ELMTREE CT

PUMP LA

MDW

LINK RD

Stockings Wood

HILL

SIBLEY'S RISE

Sibley's Coppice

2

GRIMMS HILL

GRIMMS HILL

THE AYLESBURY

WALNUT CL

MISSENDEN RD

FRITH HILL

FRITH

FRITH MILL LANE

Cudsden's Farm

CHESH

Tennis Courts

Hall
Liby

Rec Grnd

School

BURYFIELD LA

LONDON RD

THE SQ

FRITH HILL

B485 ROAD

CHESHAM

GREAT MISSENDEN

BERNARDS CL

CHILTERN MANOR PARK

STATION APPROACH

HIGH STREET

TRAFFORD CL

MISSENDEN MEWS

ABBEY WK

CHURCH STREET

Fire Station

Abbey Park

3

Great Missenden

TWITCHELL RD

WRIGHTS CL

SWAN CTTS

BACK LANE

CHURCH LANE

Missenden Abbey (College)

Squires Plantaton

TRAFFORD ROAD

WHITEFIELD

HOBBSHILL RD

MISBOURNE

LONDON ROAD

Warren Water

Rook Wood

Middle Wood

Darvells Grove

Angling Spring Farm

Abbey Park

School

Playing Field

River Misbourne

Castle Plantati

Wendover Woods

Pike Hill

4

Hobbshill Wood

The Castle

Longs Plantation

ROOK WOOD WY

ROOK WOOD WY

Tennis Courts & Club

Banks Pond

BY

5

Sedges Farm

SYLVIA CL

NAGS HEAD LANE

THE CHILTERN HOSPITAL

ROAD

Stonyrock Plantation

HEAD

Golf Course

PASS

A413

Inisfree Farm

Deep Mill Farm

HYDE LA

LANE PINES CL

NEW ROAD

REYNERS GRN

LONGFIELD

WINDSOR

WYCHWOOD RISE

DEER MEAD

ROAD

LARCH WOOD

HARE LA

Little Kingshill

6

WYCHWOOD

Wychwood Farm

HARE LANE END

NEW ROAD

NEW

LANE

LANE HARE

LANE

DEEP MILL LANE

Sandwich Wood

STONY LA

GS

E   **F**   13   **G**   **H**

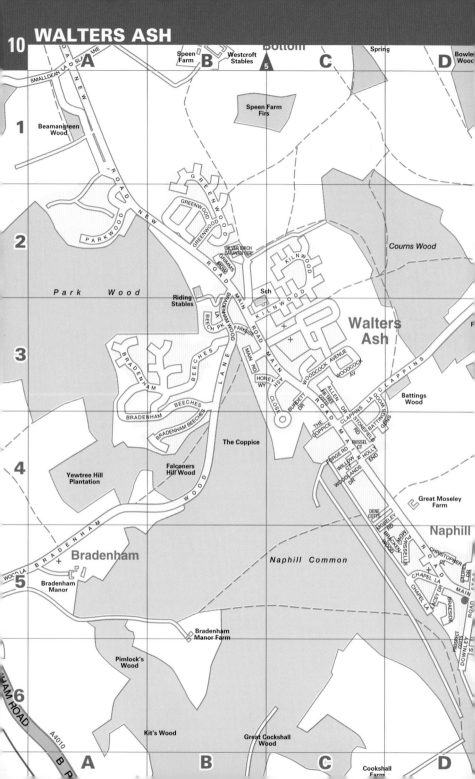

A **B** **C** **D**

Bottom

Speen Farm
Westcroft Stables
Spring
Bowled Wood

SMALLDEAN LA
SLA LANE
NEW

Speen Farm Firs

1 Beamangreen Wood

GREENWOOD

GREENWOOD

ROAD

NEW

PARKWOOD

Courns Wood

2
SILVER BIRCH CARAVAN SITE
GRIMMS MDW
KILNWOOD
KILNWOOD

Park   Wood

Riding Stables
Sch
BRADENHAM WOOD
MAIN ROAD

LA PK
BEECH
PARKSIDE

Walters Ash

3
BRADENHAM
BEECHES
MAIN RD
LANE
MAIN
ROAD
ASH
HONEY WY
CLOSE
BURDETT DR
WOODCOCK AVENUE
WOODCOCK AV
CLAPPINS

BRADENHAM BEECHES

Battings Wood

BRADENHAM BEECHES
The Coppice
WOOD
ALLEN DR
ELLER DR
ROAD
THE COPPICE
CLAPPINS LA
STONE FIELD
RUSE RD
BATTINGS
GDNS

Falconers Hill Wood
FORGE RD
RUSSEL CT
WILLOW Z HOLLY
END

4
Yewtree Hill Plantation
WOOD
WOODLANDS DR
DENE COTTS

Great Moseley Farm

MOSELEY RD
BRACKEN
WOOD
MDW
PASSELLS
R

Naphill

5
WOOD LA
BRADENHAM
Bradenham
Naphill Common
CHAPEL LA
CHAPEL LA
CHRISTOPHER CL
OTTRELL CL
MAIN
BRAESIDE
LVERY DR
PROSPECT COTTS
DOWNLEY
ROAD

Bradenham Manor

Bradenham Manor Farm

6
HAM ROAD
A4010
Pimlock's Wood

Kit's Wood
Great Cockshall Wood
Cookshall Farm

A **B** **C** **D**

E   F   G   H

Acrehill Wood

Dennerhill House

New House Farm

HAMPDEN ROAD

PERKS   LANE   PERKS

1

achdean Farm & Dairies

BRYANTS

Piggotts

Longfield Wood

North Farm

PIGGOTTS HILL

Upper North Dean

Man's Leg Wood

2

BOTTOM

MARGARET COTTS ROAD PRIMROSE COTTS

Upper Warren Farm

Hatches Wood

12

DEANFIELD COTTS SPEEN

Sherwood Farm

ROAD

HAMPDEN

Home Farm

Oakleaf Farm

Lower Warren Farm

Juniper Hill Plantation

3

Lower North Dean

BRAMLEY END

ROAD

HATCHES

LANE

TC

Little Stocking Wood

ROAD

SPEEN

LANE

WARRENDENE ROAD

Longrove Plantations

School

4

KING

Timber Research and Development Centre

Little Stocking Plantation

ROAD

SOUTH

LANE

12

VALLEY RD CHERRY TREE CL FLEET CL SPRING VALLEY DR FROGMORE CL

MAUNDS

FRIARS GDNS FRIARS GDNS FRIARS GDNS

Hughenden Valley

Chalkpit Wood

Sch

ORCHARD CL

VALLEY

Boss Lane Farm

BOSS LANE

Gomms Wood

Cry Pla

5

TREES ROAD

TREES AVENUE

ROAD

BOSS LANE

Provost Wood

A4128

CRYERS HILL ROAD CR

6

OAKESHOTT AV TYCHEN- DEN CL BAYLEY GDNS

THE ORCHARD

ROAD

Coombe Farm

COOMBE

WEDGWOOD DR COOMBE GDNS

VALLEY ROAD

rough rm

WELLHOUSE WAY LANE HILL HUNTS

Naphill Farm

CHURCH LA

BURNHAM RD WHITFIELD RD

Hall

Playing Field

V R A4128

E   F   **15**   G   H

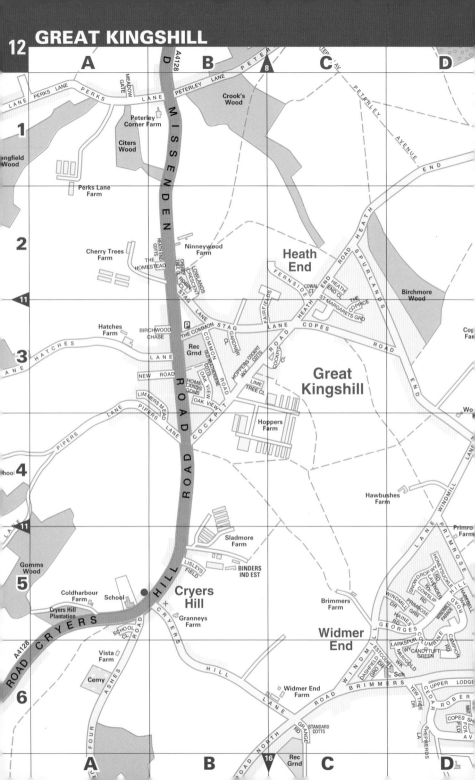

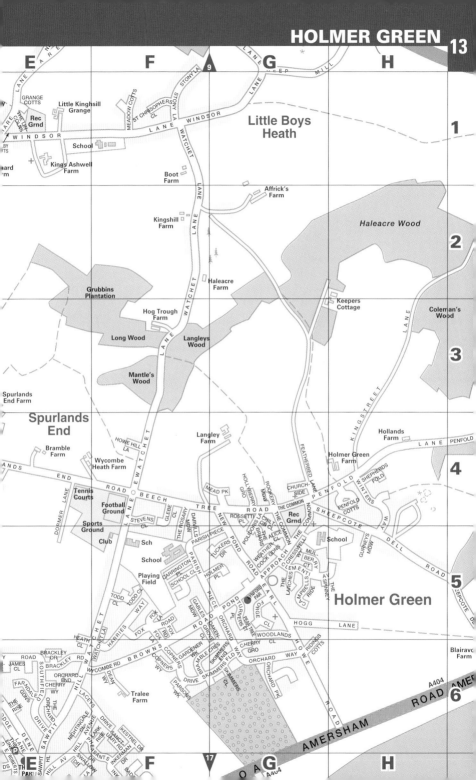

E   F   9   G   H

Little Boys
Heath

GRANGE
COTTS
Little Kinghsill
Grange
Rec
Grnd
WINDSOR
School
Kings Ashwell
Farm

Boot
Farm

Affrick's
Farm

Haleacre Wood

Kingshill
Farm

1

Grubbins
Plantation

Haleacre
Farm

Hog Trough
Farm

Long Wood

Langleys
Wood

Keepers
Cottage

Coleman's
Wood

2

Mantle's
Wood

Spurlands
End Farm

3

Spurlands
End

HOWE HILL
LA

Bramble
Farm

Wycombe
Heath Farm

Langley
Farm

Hollands
Farm

Holmer Green
Farm

SHEPHERDS
FOLD

LANE   PENFOLD

4

Tennis
Courts
Football
Ground

Sports
Ground

Club

ROAD
BEECH
Sch
School
Playing
Field

MEAD PK
TREE   ROAD
DARVILLS
GLEBE CL
STEVENS CL
THE ROSARY
PARISH   SCHOOL CL
CARRINGTON
PARISH PIECE
TUCKERS
DR
HOLMER
PL

HOLLYBERRY
GRO
ROOKERY
MDW
ROSSETTI
PL
POLDENS
COCK LANE
BRIARS
THE COMMON
THE ALICE
WEATHER
THE
CRESSWELL
APPROACH

CHURCH
SIDE
Rec
Grnd
PENFOLD
COTTS
SHEEPCOTE
THE
CLEMENT
THE
LARCHES
MBER
CT
MCBELLS
PRIDE

GURNEY'S
MDW

School

DELL

ROAD

5

Holmer Green

TODD
CL
TODD CL
WAY
FOX
ROAD
FOX
FOX CTS

HEATH
CL
HARRIES
GABLES
MDW
PIECE
ROAD
OAKEN
GRO
POND
BURKES
END
YEWFORD
PL
FORGE
CL
THE
ASPHNEY

WOODLANDS

HOGG   LANE
HOWE
RIDINGS
COTTS

BRACKLEY
DR
BRACKLEY
JAMES
CL
SOUTHFIELD
ORCHARD
END
CHERRY
WY
THE
ORCHARD

WYCOMBE RD
BROWNS
COPNERS
DEN
WY
GARDENER
COPNERS
DRIVE
ABLE CRES
BRIER

SKIMMERS
CHERRY
GRO
ORCHARD   WAY
ORCHARD PK

Blairave
Farm

Tralee
Farm

NIGHTINGALE
DRIVE
SAWPIT
HILL
HILL   AV
SWALLOW
AVENUE
PHEASANT
RISE
KESTREL DR
JARVIS RD
INKERMAN
DR

SKIMMERS FLD WY
SKIMMERS
CL
PARSONS
WK

A404
ROAD
AMERSHAM   ROAD   MER

6

E   F   17   G   H
A404

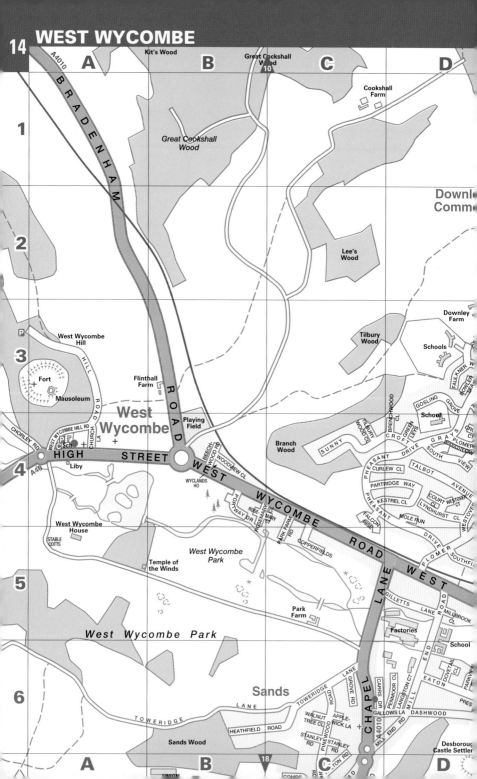

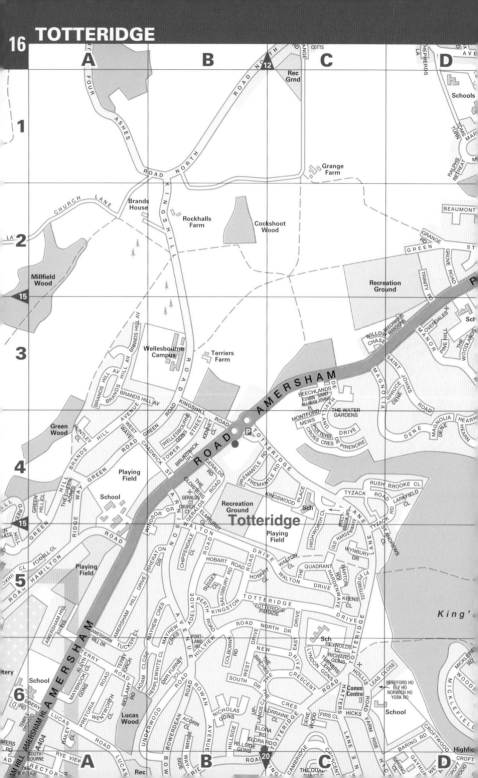

E   F   G   AMERSHAM   H

Penn Wood

1

Inkerman Farm

Two Sisters Plantation

Gravelly Way Plantation

Golf Course

Hazlemere

2

Club House

Craig's Wood

PENN ROAD

3

PENN ROAD

HAZLEMERE ROAD

Common Wood

School

The Larches

Tyler's Green

4

Recreation Ground

WEST AVENUE

CHEPPING

KINGSWOOD RD

Potter's Cross

Pugh's Wood

LANE COMMON

WOOD

5

NEW ROAD

Cricket Ground

Football Ground

Puttenham Place Farm

Community Centre

Council Offices & Depot

Sch

Hall

6

School

Playing Field

School

Penn

B474

CHURCH ROAD

E   F   G   H

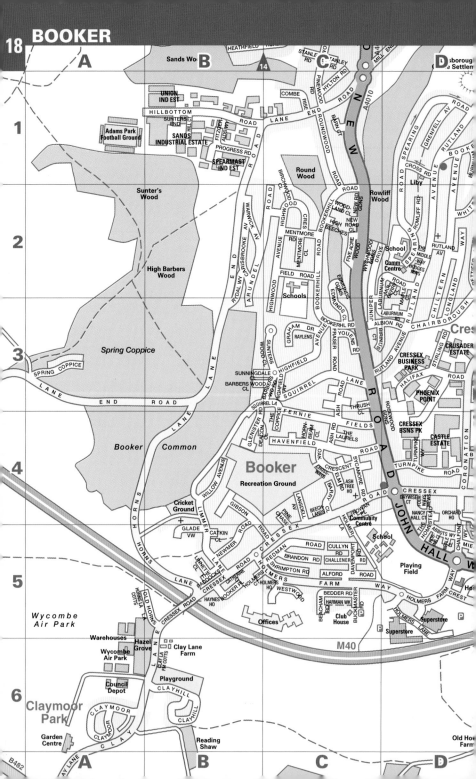

A **B** **C** **D**

HEATHFIELD

Sands Wood

14

STANLEY RD

STANLEY RD

sborough Settlem

1

UNION IND EST

HILLBOTTOM

SUNTERS END

SANDS INDUSTRIAL ESTATE

FITZGER ...RD

PROGRESS RD

SPEARMAST IND EST

Adams Park Football Ground

COMBE

PINEWOOD RD

HYLTON RD

RISE

ROUNDWOOD

BARN CT

NEW RD

MILL END ROAD

A4010

GRENFELL AV

SPEARING ROAD

CROSS RD

RUTLAND ROAD

BOOKE

AVENUE

Liby

WHIT

Round Wood

BOOKERHILL

WOOD LAND CL

HIGH BEECHES

NEW RD

NEW ROAD

FIVE ACRE WOOD

Rowliff Wood

School

Comm Centre

THE MIDDLE WAY

HODGES RNNS

RUTLAND AV

2

Sunter's Wood

High Barbers Wood

WIDMONK WY

CRISBROOKE AV

ARUNDEL

ROAD

HIGHWOOD

HIGHWOOD

AVENUE

BROWNWOOD

CRES

MENTMORE

MENTMORE CL

FIELD ROAD

Schools

BOOKERHILL

ROAD

EDMUNDS GDNS

EDMUNDS CL

FRASER RD

WYCHWOOD GDNS

DRIVE

JUNIPER

LABURNUM

MAPLE

LABURNUM RD

ALBION RD

RUTLAND

CT

ROAD

CHAIRBOROUGH

LONGLAND

CHILTERN

Cres

3

Spring Coppice

SPRING COPPICE

LANE END ROAD

RYDAL WY

SUNTERS

ROOM

HIGHFIELD

SUNNINGDALE

BARBERS WOOD CL

HIGHFIELD

SQUIRREL LA

SQUIRREL RD

GLENISTER RD

DEACON

THE COPPICE

FERNIE

HORN-BEAM CL

HAVENFIELD

GRAHAM DR

RAYLENS

BOOKERHL RD

YOUENS RD

AVENUE

ROAD

LANE

ASH RD

THRUSH

THE LAURELS

OAK

THE FIELDS

ROSEWOOD GDNS

ROAD

R O A D

HALIFAX

STIRLING RD

CRUSADER ESTATE

CRESSEX BUSINESS PARK

PHOENIX POINT

CRESSEX BSNS PK

CASTLE ESTATE

ROAD

4

Booker Common

Booker

Recreation Ground

Cricket Ground

GLADE VW

CATKIN CL

WILLOW AVENUE

HORNS

GIBSON

LIMMER ROAD

NEWMER ROAD

LANSDELL

PINE CL

CRESSEX

PAINE

BEECH LANDS

CRESCENT

ASH RD

SYCAMORE ROAD

BARRY RD

ELM RD

ASH TREE HO

CRESCENT

WATS

TURNPIKE

ROAD

CRESSEX

JOHN HALL

CORONATION

CLAYMIST CT

NANCY HALL CT

HOMESTEAD

ORCHARD

MIE

5

Wycombe Air Park

Warehouses

Wycombe Air Park

Hazel Grove

OLD HORNS COTTS

HORNSLA COTTS

OLD HORNS LANE

CRESSEX ROAD

CATHERINE

THE PADDOCKS

LINNER CL

HAYNES HO

BOOKER RD

C HOLMERS

WESTWOOD

FARM

CULLYN RD

BRANDON RD

REDMAN ROAD

SHRIMPTON RD

ALFORD ROAD

CHALLENER RD

DAVENPORT RD

BEDDER RD

HARMAN WK

BUCKMASTER RD

Club House

WAY

Community Centre

School

Playing Field

HOLMERS LANE

HOLMERS

Superstore

FARM CREST

WAY

Hos

6

Claymoor Park

Council Depot

CLAYHILL

CLAY FLAT COTTS

Clay Lane Farm

Playground

CLAYHILL

CLAYHILL

CLAYMOOR ROAD

CLAY

AY LANE

B482

Garden Centre

Reading Shaw

M40

Superstore

Offices

Old Ho Farm

A **B** **C** **D**

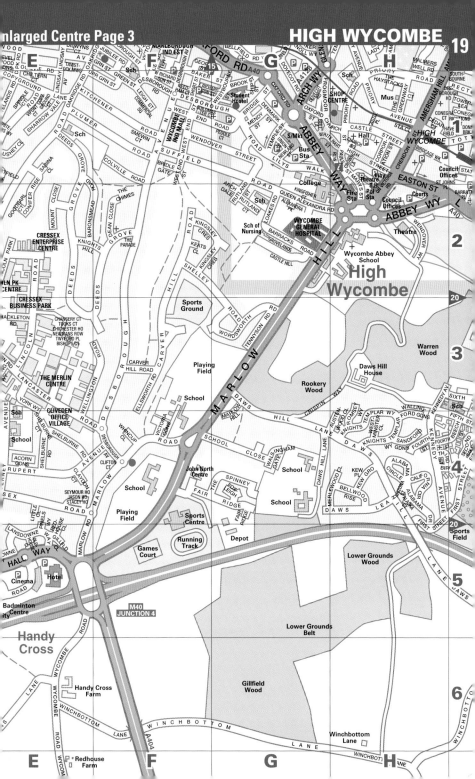

High Wycombe

Handy Cross

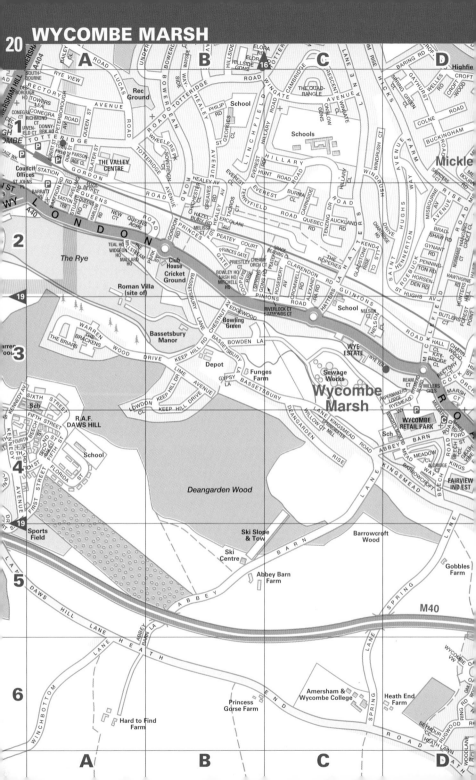

Grid labels (top): E F G H

Grid labels (right side): 1 2 3 4 5 6

Labels visible on map:

- ROAD
- School
- B474
- CHURCH ROAD
- SANDPITS LANE
- HAMMER LA
- HILL
- STUMPWELL LANE
- Liby
- PLANTATION RD
- ULANDS VW
- HERBERT ROAD
- Pastures Farm
- Gomm's Wood
- Little Gomm's Wood
- The Danes
- Pond Wood
- BEACON
- GROVE
- PIMMS CL
- LINGWOODWAY CL
- PIMMS
- Town Farm
- Bottom Farm
- Golf Course
- Co... H...
- PEREGRINE BUSINESS PARK
- Riding School
- Magpie Wood
- CLEARBROOK CL
- THE RISE
- HAMMERSLEY LA
- SALTASH CL
- TAMAR CL
- CLEARBROOK CL
- Club House
- Lude Farm
- Works
- PLACE
- LUDLOW MEWS
- PENT-LANDS
- WR MM-
- HAMMERSLEY LA
- DUNKELD RD
- BRAMBLE
- LAUREL
- ROBINSON WAY
- WALKHAM WAY
- WINCHESTER
- AVENUE
- Sniggs Wood
- Wks
- LONDON
- GARDEN
- DRIVE
- CL...
- MAGHE
- ROAD
- MOBILE HOME PARK
- RAYNERS CL
- 22
- Kings Mead
- Club
- RIVERSWOOD GDNS
- LONDON RD
- ROSEBANK
- WHINNEYS
- KINGSMEAD OFFICE CAMPUS
- FREDERICK
- Sports Field
- DEREHAMS LA
- Upper Dearham's Farm
- BRIDGE
- HOLLY CL
- DOLPHIN
- THE SKINS
- MALLARD PL
- GROVE
- SCHOOL
- NORWOOD CL
- Depot
- ST ANNS
- DEREHAMS
- ALTONA RD
- Altona Road
- Cemy
- Loudwater
- Fennells Wood
- Sch
- FASSETT
- LITTON CL
- IMPERIAL CT
- QUEENS MEAD HO
- BLAKES HO
- EBENEZER
- THE STEAD COPSE
- THORNE
- BAY TREE CL
- BRANCH RD
- QUEENSMEAD RD
- SEVEN ACRE HO
- OLD FORGE
- GRIFFITH HO
- BROOK HO
- CHILTERN CL
- BIRFIELD RD
- BERKELEY RD
- P.H.
- Hotel
- WINDSOR CRES
- White House
- WAY OAKLAND WAY
- FENNEL
- Fennells Wood
- Beechwood Hall
- WILLOW OAK
- BROOK-SIDE
- ST PETERS
- CASCO CL
- ADA
- CONWAY CL
- THAMESTEAD
- A40
- KNAVES BEECH IND EST
- TREADAWAY BSNS CENTRE
- BOUNDARY
- BLAKELEY RD
- 24
- STATION ROAD
- CH WY
- A4094
- Supermarket
- H/ooburn M...
- Fennells Wood

Grid navigation markers: 17, 22, 24

Forty Green

Holtspur

Wooburn
Green

THE MERCURY PARK

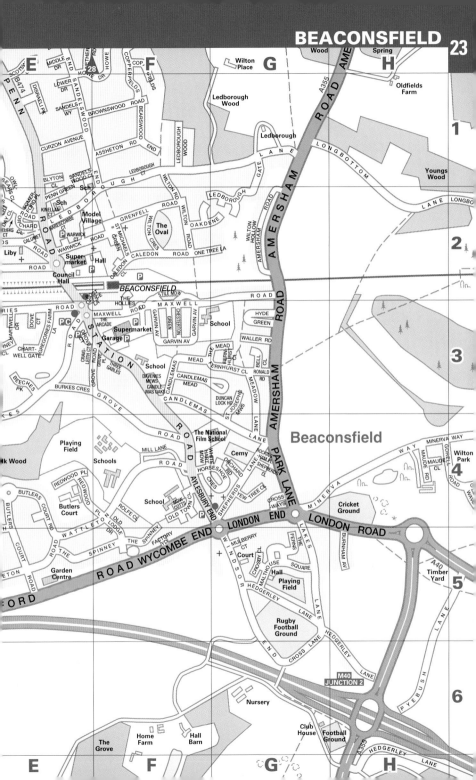

Beaconsfield

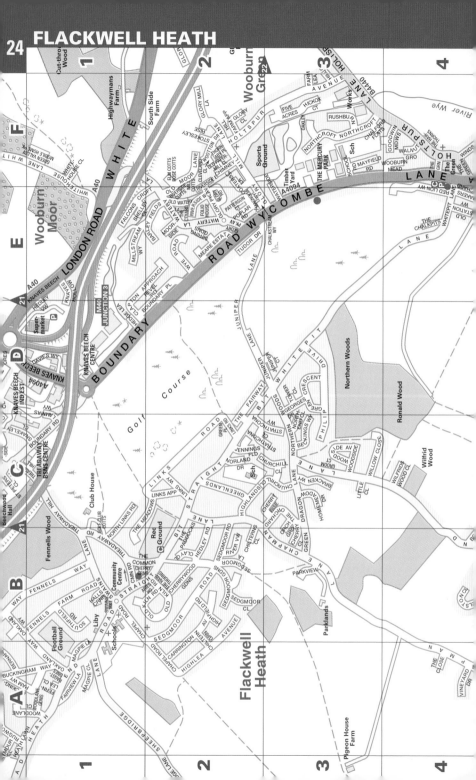

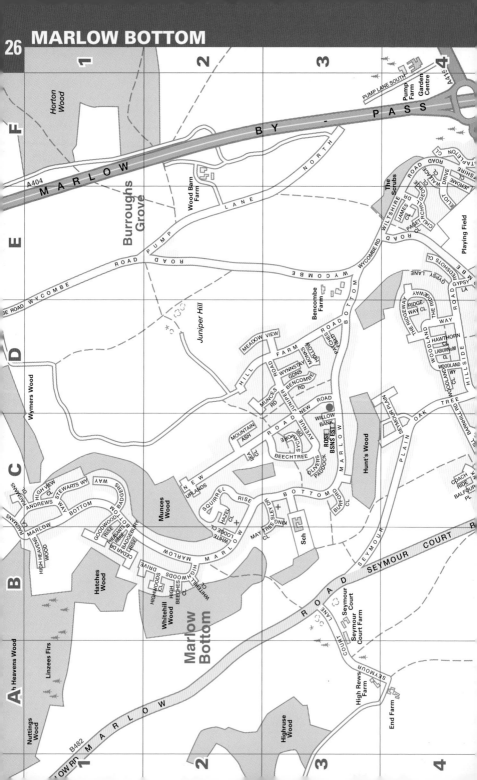

Horton Wood

MARLOW A404 BY-PASS NORTH

PUMP LANE SOUTH

Pump Farm

Garden Centre

A4155

Burroughs Grove

Wood Barn Farm

PUMP LANE

ROAD ROAD WYCOMBE ROAD

WYCOMBE WYCOMBE ROAD

BE ROAD WYCOMBE

The Scrubs

WILTSHIRE ROAD

VILLAGE RD SHIRE ROAD JEROME CL

JEROME DRIVE

PAGET CL GEO RICH CHURCH CL ELIOT CL JAMES CL

TAPLETON ROAD

Playing Field

GYPSY LANE

GYPSY LA

REDSHOTS CL

THE RIDGEWAY

THE RIDGE WAY CL

WOODLAND WAY

HAWTHORN CL LABURNUM CL

WOODLAND CL WOODLAND WY

WOODLAND HILLSIDE

Juniper Hill

Bencombe Farm

ROAD BOTTOM PEACHES

HILL

MEADOW VIEW

FARM ROAD

WYNNSTAY GDNS

JUNIPER BENCOMBE RD

WINDSOR CL

Wymers Wood

MUNCES RD

ROAD

NEW ROAD

WILLOW BANK

TREE OAK

SYCAMORE AVENUE

ROSE BSNS EST

MARLOW

SEYMOUR PLAIN

PLAIN

MOUNTAIN ASH

BEECHTREE

OLIVERS PADDOCK

OLD BURFORD CL

Hunt's Wood

COACH RIDE BALFOUR PL

High Heavens Wood

Linzees Firs

High View CL ANDREWS WAY STEWARTS WY

FAGMANS

MARLOW BOTTOM

WY WOODBADGERS

RISE

GOODWOOD RISE

FRIARS RISE SADGEBURY

CEDAR RD RISE

NEW UPLANDS

Munces Wood

SQUIRREL RISE

HAZEL WHITE LODGE CL

KING SLEY

MAY TREE CL

NEW ROAD

Sch

Nuttings Wood

B482

LOW RD MARLOW RD

Hatches Wood

HIGH HEAVENS WOOD

MARLOW BOTTOM

DRIVE HIGHWOODS CL

WHITEHILL HIGH BEECHES CL

Whitehill Wood

Marlow Bottom

Highruse Wood

ROAD

SEYMOUR COURT

SEYMOUR COURT LANE

Seymour Court

Seymour Court Farm

SEYMOUR COURT

High Rews Farm

End Farm

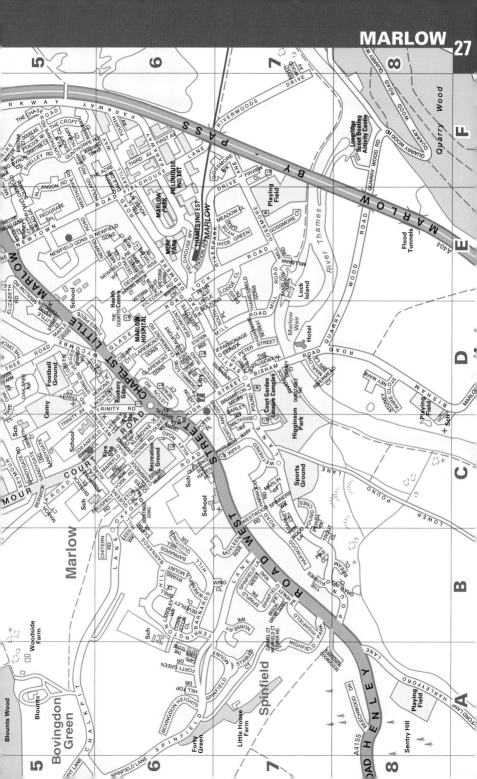

Marlow

Bovingdon
Green

Blounts Wood

Woodside
Farm

Spinfield

Sentry Hill

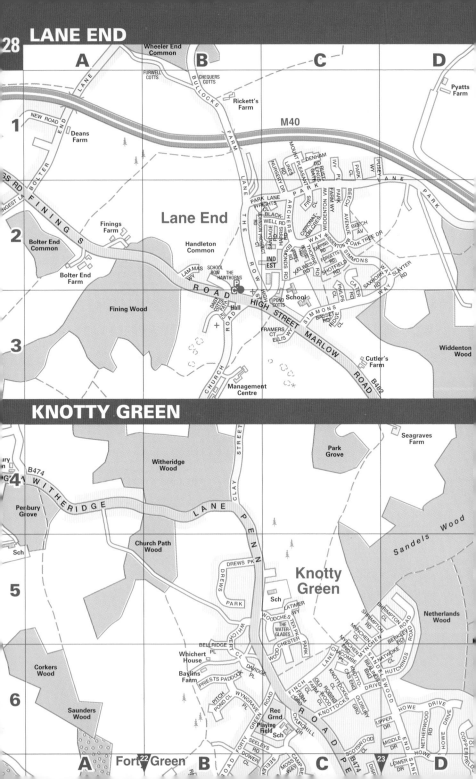

LANE END

Wheeler End Common

A   B   C   D

FURWELL COTTS
CHEQUERS COTTS
Rickett's Farm
Pyatts Farm

NEW ROAD
M40

1

Deans Farm

BOLTER END LANE
FININGS RD
LONGEST LA

Finings Farm

Lane End

Bolter End Common

2

Handleton Common

Bolter End Farm

SCHOOL
THE HAWTHORNS
LAMMAS WY
ROW

PARK LANE
WRIGHTS RD
NURSERY DR
MOUNT PLEASANT
DENHAM RD
INGS LINES
ELMS END
IVY PL
PARK WY
BEECH
PUSEY LANE
THE ROW
BLACK-WELL RD
SANDAGE RD
SHRIMPTON RD
EDMONDS RD
PROSPECT
ARCHERS
CORONAT CLOSE
FIFE
CL
WIDMORE
THORNE RD
PIPPING RD
WIDDENTON WY
FORGETTS RD
ELWES RD
SHOTFIELD
SIMMONS
CATER RD
BEECH AVENUE
OAK TREE DR
BEECH AV
PARK FARM WY
SAXHORN RD
WAY SLAYTER
PHLPS CL
WAY

IND EST

Fining Wood

3

HIGH STREET
ROAD
CHURCH STREET
OASIS COTTS PATH
Hall
POND COTTS
SIMMONS
BASSET CL
RIDGE CL
FRAMERS CT
ELLIS WY
School
MARLOW ROAD
B482
Cutler's Farm
Widdenton Wood

Management Centre

KNOTTY GREEN

A   B   C   D

Seagraves Farm

CLAY STREET

Witheridge Wood

Park Grove

4

B474
WITHERIDGE

Penbury Grove

LANE PENN

Sandels Wood

Sch

Netherlands Wood

Church Path Wood

DREWS PK

5

DREWS PARK

Sch

Knotty Green

LATIMER WY
WOODCHES

SHRIMPTON CL
BERKLEY RD
MYNCHEN CL
MANCHEN RD
MYNCHEN END
CHICOMBE RD
MATTOKE RD
HUTCHINGS
SPRIMPTON RD

Corkers Wood

WHITOVER
BELLRIDGE PL
Whichert House
Baylins Farm
PRIESTS PADDOCK
THE WATER-GLADES
CHESTER
WOOD
DAVIDGE PL
FINCH
FERN
OLD ROBINS
KNOTTOCKS END
KNOTTOCKS DR
CHICOMBE
CL
CAXS END
KNOTTOCKS GRO
OLDBURY
DRIVE

6

Saunders Wood

PITCH POND CL
WYNGRAVE PL
Rec Grnd
Playing Field
GREEN ROAD
FORTY GREEN RD
SEELEYS RD
DOWER CL
MOSS CL
CAMP BE
CHURCHILL ROAD
Sch
HOWE DR
UPPER DR
MIDDLE DR
LOWER SAN
NETHERWOOD DR
HOWE DRIVE
HOWE DR
SCOTSWOOD
B474

A   **Forty Green**   B   C   D

22   23

A   B   C   D

Hydehouse Plantation

Hyde Heath Common

White's Wood

Monk's Wood

1

HEATH LANE

BULLBAITERS LANE

Hyde Heath Farm

BROMLEY LA

HEATH LANE

WEEDON

Sch

Nursing Home

Hyde Heath

2

CEDAR RIDGE

SAUNDERS END

BRAYS RIDGE

POND COTTS

BRAYS CL

WY

MEADOW END

BRAY'S MEADOW

WESTFIELD

HARVEST BANK

Weedon Hill Farm

WEEDON HILL LANE

LANE

CO

BRAYS CL

BRAYS GREEN LANE

WALNUT

STONE-CROFT

KEEPERS

WAY

32

Motte & Bailey

CHALK LANE

Bray's Wood

KEEPERS LANE

COPPERKINS LANE

3

Weedonh Farm

LANE

ORCHARD RD

HIGHLANDS RD

HOWARD CRESCENT

HOWARD ROAD

ROAD

PARK PL

MANOR RD

Recreation Ground

38

LANE

4

GURNELLS RD

WYNNGSWICK RD

RAESIDE CL

GROVE

CHALFONT

HEARNES CL

HEARNES MDW

MANOR CRES

TWITCHELLS LANE

Pond

CHERRY-WOOD CL

CHURCH PADDOCKS END

DINNERS

WOOD

MANOR PKWAY

PONDCL

MOSS CT

ORCHARD MEWS

Seer Green

LANE

LANE

5

LONG BOTTOM

DROVERS

DEEP FIELD

COPSE FIELD

FARMERS WAY

CLEVERS WAY

GREEN WOOD CL

THE COPPICE

BARRACKS LA

STABLE LA

COLT LA

Manor Farm

Hall Place

Sch

Long Wood

LONG WOOD DR

MEADOWSIDE WAY

School

SCHOOL LANE

VICARAGE RD

BAYNE

BAYNE HILL CL

Cemy

SEER MEAD

SEER MEAD

Hall

SEER GREEN LANE

COPSE LANE

PUERS LANE

GREEN WEST RD

GRN NTH RD

GREEN EAST RD

CRUTCHES RD

JORDANS LANE

JORDANS LANE

JORDANS

C

LONGBOTTOM

GROVE HILL

LANE

WILLTON LA

WILTON LANE

BEECH LANE

COPSE LANE

Crutches Wood

JORDANS LANE

6

SEER GREEN & JORDANS

Club House

FARM LANE

DEAN FARM RD

LANE LONG BOTTOM LANE

Dean Farm

JONES LANE

Youth Hostel

WELDERS LANE

Spring Wood

WELDER

Stone Dea

A   B   C   D

A B C D

Bellingdon

1 Bloomfield Farm
Huge Farm
Hilltop Farm
Woodlands Farm
Woodview Farm

Widmore Wood
Johnson's Farm

White Hawridge Bottom

2 Savecroft Farm
Ramscoat Wood
Bowe Farm

3 Tiles Farm
Captain's Wood (Nature Reserve)
MEADOW CL
COPSE WY
Broadview Farm

Mount Nugent Farm
WOODCOTE LAWNS
LITTLE GANCEL CT
LITTLE GREAT HIVINGS
HIVINGS RD
BROADVIEW
G SWAN CL

4 Hazeldene Farm
Great Hivings
MARSTON CL
HOLLY-BUSH RD
REY-NOLDS WY
CHARMS WY
NUGENT CT
CAPTAINS CL
WYKERIDGE CL
HIVINGS PK
Sch
Playing Fields

BUSLINS LA
BUSLINS LANE
BUSLINS
Greenway Parade
GREENWAY
Sch
LONG MEADOWAY
POPLAR CL
ABBOTS PL
ABBOTS VALE
VALE RD

5 SAXEWAYS BSNS CENTRE
THE WARREN
THE WARREN
CHARTRIDGE LANE
Portobello Farm
CROSS MDW
LONGFIELD RD
UPPER BELMONT RD
PATTERSON RD
HOWARD RD
SPRING
Rec Grnd
LYNTON RD
GLENISTER RD
OVERDALE RD
CHILTO...

ASHERIDGE ROAD
HIVINGS CT
HILLSIDE
BELMONT
RIDGEWAY RD
WINDSOR RD
UPLAND AV
LYNHURST
WILLIAM RD
MOULDER CT
NUTKINS WY
HOWARD IND EST

6 Depot
Works
CHILTERN COMMERCIAL CENTRE
Works
DARVELL DR
DARVELL
POLES HL
POLES HILL
CHAPMANS HILL
FAIRLEA
VALLEY
BELMONT RD
RIDGEWAY WK
COWPER RD
MASER GRAYS
SHELLEY RD
MILTON RD
CHESTER-TON CL
BATCHELORS WY
MANOR RD
LANSDOWNE
HIGH-FIELD RD
ADDISON ROAD
Pond Park
VIEW
BEVAN HILL
DEANSWAY
SKIPTON
Newtown
ALMA
CEMY
HONEYSUCKLE
FIELD
Wks
CROWN BSNS EST

PEDNOR ROAD PEDNOR
Pednor Mead
BERKELEY AV
Poultry Farm
HUNTERS
PULPIT CL
GARSON GRO
AYLWARD GDNS
DELLFIELD CL
BENHAM CL
WALLIN
BEECH...
ACACIA
Sch
Fire Sta
Works
DEANSWAY
BELLINGDON RD
CHALK HILL
SUNNYSIDE

A B 32 C D

E F G H

Old Oak Farm

HOG LANE

SNOWHILL COTTS

Ashley Green

CURTIS A416

HOG LANE TWO

ROAD

1

Flamstead Farm

Hall

DELLS LANE TWO

Thorne Barton Farm

2

Thorne Barton Hall

The Warren

SUNNYSIDE COTTS

GREEN

Little Pressmore Farm

Woodside

DELLS LANE

3

Pressmore Farm

Sloelands Farm

Nashleigh Farm

Torrington Farm

E LANE

ASHLEY

Amersham & Wycombe College Chesham Campus

PARTRIDGE CL

Sch

ORCHARD LEIGH VS

GROVE LA

4

Whitehorn's Farm

SUNNYMEDE AV

TWO DELLS LA

LANE

RUSH

HILL

LYCROME

FIELD CL

ROAD

LYCROME

ROAD

RUSHMERE

B4505

LYCROME LA

WOODCROFT RD

SYCAMORE DENE

DEER PARK WK

ROAD

Lye Green

5

Lyegreen Farm

ASHLEIGH

RUSSELL CT

PRESTON HILL

CHERRY TREE WK

BIRCH WY

School

GREEN

Brockhurst Farm

HILLCROFT RD

ASHFIELD RD

BRUSHWOOD RD

NALDERS CRES

SPY WARD

BIRCH WY

ROAD

CRABBE CRES

GEST

REHAM CL

VIEW ROAD

Bayman Manor Cotts

Bayman Manor

6

STREET

FRANCES

CODMORE WY

HALL CL

TAYLORS

CAMERON RD

NALDERS WEST

THE SPINNEY

HAWTHORN WY

CHESTNUT AV

WAY MANOR WY

THE GRAND

B4505

WARRENER RD

Hilltop

ROAD

GREEN

LYE

Codmore

Sch

CODMORE CRES

CODMORE CRES

ROAD

LEE LA

WANNG

LEY LA

E F G H

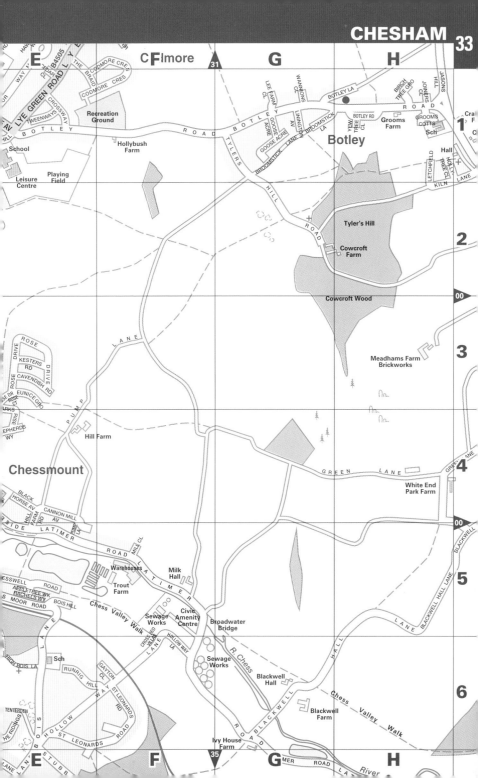

Botley

Tyler's Hill

Cowcroft
Farm

Cowcroft Wood

Meadhams Farm
Brickworks

Chessmount

White End
Park Farm

Hill Farm

GREEN LANE

Recreation
Ground

Hollybush
Farm

School

Leisure
Centre

Playing
Field

ROSE DRIVE
KESTERS RD
CAVENDISH RD
EUNICE GRO

PUMP LANE

Grooms
Farm

GROOMS
COTTS
Sch

Hall

LETCHFIELD

KILN

E F Imore G H

31

BOTLEY ROAD

TWEENWAYS
CROSSWAY
THE BRAIDS
CODMORE CRES

LEE FARM CL
GOOSE ACRE
BROOMSTICK LA
LININGTON AV
WANNONS CL

BOTLEY LA

BOTLEY RD
YEW TREE CL

BIRCH TREE GRO
JOINERS HILL
JASONS HILL
ROAD

HOLLY TREE CL
LANE

TYLERS HILL ROAD

Warehouses
Trout
Farm

Milk
Hall

MILL CL

LATIMER ROAD

Milk Hall

Civic
Amenity
Centre

Sewage
Works

Broadwater
Bridge

R. Chess

Sewage
Works

Blackwell
Hall

Blackwell
Farm

BLACKWELL ROAD

BLACKWELL HALL LANE

HALL LANE

GREEN LANE

Chess Valley Walk

BLACK HORSE AV
HILL FARM AV
CANNON MILL AV
LATIMER

CRESSWELL ROAD
APPLETREE WK
RACHELS WY
BOIS HILL
MOOR ROAD

Chess Valley Walk

CROSSHILL LANE
HOLLOW WAY
LA

Sch
RUNRIG HILL
GAYTON CL
ST LEONARDS RD

HIGH BOIS LA

TENTERDEN
THE RIDINGS

BOIS LANE
HOLLOW WAY
ST LEONARDS ROAD
STUBBS

Ivy House
Farm

E F G H

35

MER ROAD

River
LANE

1

2

00

3

4

00

5

6

LYE GREEN ROAD
B4505
HAW LA
WAY
CEDAR AV
THE

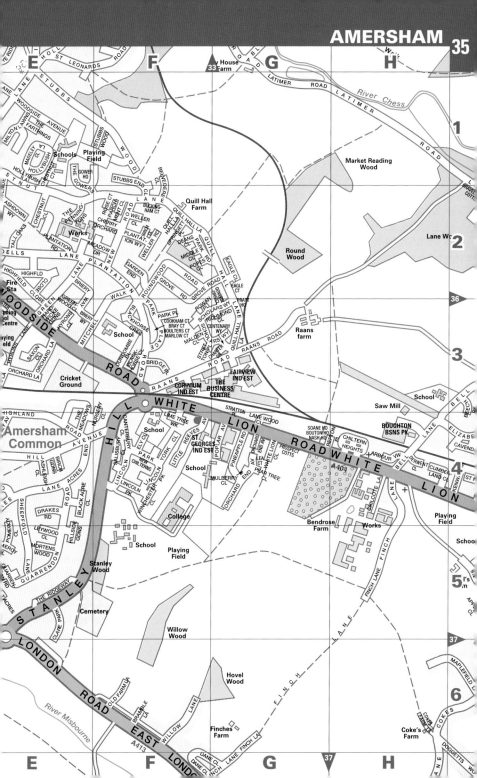

Baldwin's Wood

Gearys Plantation

Flaunden Grove

The Home Farm

Latimer

Chenies Bottom

Coney Wood

Walk Wood

R. Chess

ROAD LATIMER

STONY LANE

STONY LA

CHURCH GRO

Greathouse Farm

A404

ROAD AME

Old Hanging Wood

LODGE

THE RETREAT

GROVE

AVENUE

CHURCH WAY

OLD FIELD CL

OAKINGTON

School

Stockings Spring

Socks Spring

FLAUNDEN BOTTOM

FLAUNDEN

STONY

Lower Water

ROAD LATIMER

LANE

CHESSFIELD PARK

CHESSFIELD

WESTWOOD

AMERSHAM

CL

CODMORE WOOD RD

WOOD RD

CODMORE WOOD ROAD

THE RIDINGS

SPRING CL

THE

THE GROVE

GROVE

Parkfield Wood

Latimer House

West Wood

Westwood Park Sports Field

DRIVE

AV

CHALFONT

AVENUE

WESTWOOD

RUSSELL

BEDFORD

BEDFORD AVENUE

CHENIES AV

Latimer Park Farm

Great Water

Latimer Park

ROAD LATIMER LANE

BELL LANE

BEECHWOOD AVENUE

BROUGHTON W

PAVILION WY

ELIZABETH CL

CHENIES

BEECHWOOD

FARM RD

AVENUE

CL

CHALFONT & LATIMER STA

CHALFONT & LATIMER STATION RD

APPLE

AMERSHAM

VILLAGE WY

LATIMER CL

LOUDHAMS RD

Duck Cover

Ladies Arbour

BELL LANE

CHANDS CL

SANDYCROFT ROAD

KILN AV

CHARSLEY CL

ELIZABETH AVENUE

CAVENDISH CL

MARYGOLD WK

CLAYTON

BEEL CL

Snell's

ROAD

LION

Lane Wood

River Chess

ROAD LATIMER

BRIMMELL COTTS

THE BEECHES

BEECH PK

ELIZABETH CL

LAND CL

DERWENT WY

KENWAY RD

ST NICHOLAS

Playing Field

33

Walk

Market Reading Wood

Saw Mill

School

BOUGHTON BSNS PK

LANE BELL

CHILCOTE LANE

CHILTERN HEIGHTS

ARBOUR

CANE HO

AUTUMN HO

WASH HO

ROAD ADWHITE

A404

Works

endrose Farm

Chorleywood West

Newhouse Farm

Hillas Wood

Roughwood Park

Lodge Copse

Lodge Farm

Crosslane Wood

Roughwood Farm

ROUGHWOOD

NEW RD

LODGE LANE

LANE

BURTON LANE

BURTONS LANE

Burton's Farm

Burton's Wood

WAY

Loudhams Wood

BURTONS LANE

GROVE

PARK

REACH

GATE

BIRKETT WY

LOUDHAMS WK

YARROWSIDE

BURTONS WAY

HAREWOOD RD

HAREWOOD RD

HAREWOOD LANE

FIELDS

APPLETON CL

NIGHTINGALES LANE

NIGHTINGALES LANE

B4442

Warren Farm

WARREN FARM COTTS

NIGHTINGALES

COKES LANE

DOGGETTS WOOD LANE

DOGGETTS WOOD CL

MAPLEFIELD LA

COKES LANE

COKE'S FARM LANE

Doggett's Farm

Pollards Park House

Pollards Park House

Coke's Farm

Club House

P o l l a r d s   W o o d

G o l f   C o u r s e

Harewood Downs House

A413

A413 AMERSHAM ROAD A M

HOUSE FARM

COKES LANE

LANE

39

38

35

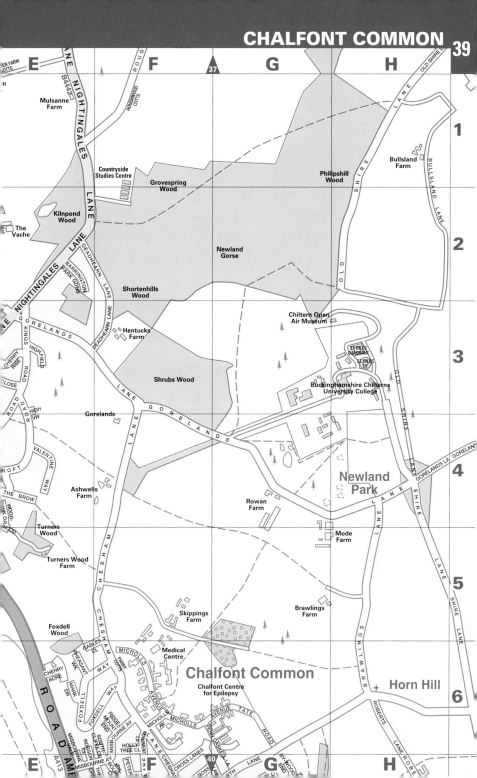

E F 37 G H

Mulsanne
Farm

B4442

NIGHTINGALES LANE

ROUGH

ROUGHWOOD COTTS

Countryside
Studies Centre

Grovespring
Wood

Philipshill
Wood

OLD SHIRE LANE

Bullsland
Farm

BULLSLAND LANE

1

Kilnpond
Wood

The
Vache

NIGHTINGALES LANE

BARRINGTON

PARK GDNS

DEADHEARN LANE

Newland
Gorse

OLD

SHIRE

2

GORELANDS

KINGS ROAD

HIGHFIELD

CHERRY RISE

CLOSE

ROAD

HIGH VW

Shortenhills
Wood

Hentucks
Farm

Chiltern Open
Air Museum

ST GILES QUADRANT

ST GILES CT

3

LANE

GORELANDS

Shrubs Wood

Buckinghamshire Chilterns
University College

OLD

SHIRE

LANE

Gorelands

VALENTINE WAY

CROFT

THE BROW

WOOD

PARK DRIVE

WOOD

Ashwells
Farm

Rowan
Farm

Newland
Park

GORELANDS LA. GORELAN

SHIRE LANE

4

Turners
Wood

Turners Wood
Farm

CHESHAM

Mode
Farm

LANE

5

Foxdell
Wood

GABLES CL

PHEASANT WK

CHERRY ACRE

MARK DR

CHESHAM

WAY

MICHOLLS PARK

Skippings
Farm

Medical
Centre

Brawlings
Farm

BRAWLINGS

SHIRE LANE

ROAD

A413

FOXDELL WAY

RIDGE MOUNT

MISBOURNE AV

CLIFFE

SOUTH

ROBSON

MISBOURNE AV

HOLLY TREE CL

PETER

AVENUE

MICHOLLS AV

LANE

MICHOLLS

CHESHAM

PENN CASKELLA

CROSS LANES

AVENUE

NORTH

TATE

PENWOOD END

ROAD

ROBERTS

LANE ROBE

Chalfont Common

Chalfont Centre
for Epilepsy

Horn Hill

6

E F 40 G H

CHALFONT ST PETER

Roberts Farm
Roberts Lane
Roberts Wood
WEST HYDE LANE
Bloom Wood
Round Pocker Plantation
HYDE LANE
WEST
Warren Farm
Chalfont Heights Scout Camp
Mopes LA
South Bucks Way
Hogtrough Wood
BY-WOODS END
NORTOFT RD
COPPER RIDGE
COPPER DR
RIDGE WOOD
ROAD
Rec Grnd
Cemy
Sch
DENHAM LANE
WINKERS LA
WINKERS WY
MORRIS CL
THE WARREN
HILL
ROAD
NINNINGS
Sch
39
CROSS LANES
CEDARS CL
LA LANE END
RAVENSMEAD
DENHAM
DENHAM WK
HIGHLANDS
HIGHLANDS END
HIGHLANDS LA
GLYNSWOOD
COPTHALL
JOINERS
ROYLE CL
THE DRIVE
CHESTNUT
HILLGROVE
ELLIS
AVENUE
LEWIS LA
CHILTERN
LINCOLN
ROADSIDE
LINDEN DRIVE
CHILTERN RISE
DEANCROFT RD
GARNERS RD
GARNERS END
GARNERS CL
NICHOLAS CL
BUCKINGHAM RD
THE BRAMBLES
HEDGEROW
LLANVAIR DR
FARM RD
COPTHALL CORNER
WHITE HOUSE CL
HILLFIELD
ROAD
CHESTNUT WK
JOINERS CL
ST PETERS CL
SANDY RISE
MONUMENT LANE
MOORTOWN RD
CHESHAM LANE
PHYGTLE
THE SHELL
OLD MEAD
WHEATLEY WAY
HILLSIDE CL
FRICKMANSWORTH
WHEELERS ORCH
ROBINS ORCHD
GRAVEL HILL
COPTHALL
ROAD
GRASSINGHAM END
BEACON CT
GRASSINGHAM RD
ST PETERS
HIGH ST
HILION CRES
CRES
GRANGE DR
GRANGE RD
BRANCH RD
WOODSIDE
HIGHER MOW
FIELDS CL
HILL RISE
HILL RISE CRES
WOODCROFT
HOLLY TREE CL
PETER CL
MONUMENT LANE
SOUTHCLIFFE CL
BOURNE CL
ROBSON CL
THE DREY
PADDOCK
DEANACRE CL
COOKS
THE BELL
Pol Sta
ELMS RD
Comm Centre
PENN RD CHURCH LANE
ROBSONS NEWS
Sch
ROAD
Amb Sta
Convent
MISBOURNE
MONUMENT LANE
AMERSHAM RD
A413
GRAVEL HILL
Chalfont St Peter F.C.
FIELDWAY
PENN ROAD
THE LAUREL CL
WINDMILL ROAD
LANSDOWN RD
HAMPDEN RD
HIGH ST
MARKET PLACE
CHURCHFIELD RD
VALE RD
PARK ROAD
GROVE
CONVENT
CHERRYTREE LA
GOLD HILL EAST
Bowstridge
Windmill Farm
Woodlands Farm
Sch
BOUNDARY RD
OUT-LAND RD
PENNINGTON RD
TOPLAND RD
GLEBE CL
LOVEL ROAD
LOVEL END
LOVEL MEAD
LOVEL GROVE
GROVE END
ELEANOR RD
NICOL CL
ROAD GROVE
THE CHALFONTS & GERRARDS CROSS HOSPITAL
Leisure Centre
College
NICOL END
GOLD HILL
GOLDHILL CROFT
ORCHARD GRO
FRIARS CL
CHARD GRO
MAYVEN
GOLD HILL WEST
BENCH MANOR CRES
CLOSE
LAYTERS END
Goldhill Common
BOWSTRIDGE LANE
NARCOT LANE
TUNMERS END
NARCOT LANE
WELDERS LANE
LEACHCROFT
WEEDON CL
LEACHCROFT
NICOL GROVE
CHIPSTEAD CL
CHALFONT GROVE LANE
POND LANE
POND LANE
LAYTERS GREEN LANE
LAYTERS CLOSE
LAYTERS
Layters Green Farm
Bramleys Farm
BOWSTRIDGE LANE
Outfield Plantation
NARCOT LANE
Layters Green

The Index includes some names for which there is insufficient space on the maps. These names are indicated by an * and are followed by the nearest adjoining thoroughfare.

leside HP11 21 E4
ey End HP14 11 G3
ton Mews SL7 27 D7
Rd HP10 21 F6
on Rd HP12 18 C5
s Hill Av HP13 16 A4
ngs La SL9 39 H6
t HP6 35 F3
CI HP6 29 B2
Green La HP6 29 B3
La HP6 29 B2
Mdw HP6 29 B2
CI SL7 27 B8
n Way HP13 15 E5
wood CI HP13 14 D4
Rd SL8 25 B6
vood HP15 17 F2
vood CI HP14 6 B4
ell Walk HP15 17 F3
Bank CI HP11 21 E5
PI HP6 35 F3
St HP11 3 A4
stone Dr SL8 25 C6
Gate HP11 19 F1
Way HP6 35 E2
SL7 27 B6
ers Hill HP15 12 C6
ers Rd HP27 4 C5
es La HP9 22 B1
ey Av HP13 15 F5
Hurst SL7 27 C6
n Ct SL7 27 F5
nia Rd HP5 30 D6
Ct HP14 6 C5
La,
ne End HP10 25 E7
La,
ourn Green
22 C6
Leys HP27 4 A4
st HP5 32 C1
ands Av HP5 32 D1
View HP5 30 C4
way CI HP7 34 C5
urst Rd HP6 31 E6
ey La HP6 29 B2
St HP11 3 A3
bank HP10 25 D6
e Furmston PI
27 D5
e Rd HP27 4 B4
ield Rd HP10 25 D6
house Dr HP10 25 D6
side HP10 21 F6
CI HP15 17 E2
barn La HP16 8 C3
field CI HP16 8 D2
afield Hill HP16 8 D3
astick La HP5 33 G1
s Rd HP15 13 F6
swood Rd HP9 23 E1
Rd HP13 15 F5
wick PI HP13 16 B4
Makers CI HP5 32 C1
wood Rd HP5 31 F6
s Bottom Rd
11 F1
gham CI HP13 21 E1
gham Ct HP6 35 F2
gham Dr HP13 20 D1
gham PI HP13 3 A3
gham Way
20 D6
aster Rd HP12 18 C5
,
rds Cross SL9 41 C5
,
Wycombe HP11 3 B4
iters La HP6 29 A2
ks Farm La
28 B1
nd La WD3 39 H1
ode Ct SL9 41 C8
ode Way SL9 41 B7
t Dr HP14 10 C3
d CI SL7 26 C3
ss Wood Gro
22 C4
ss Wood Rd
ss Wood Rd South
22 C5
s CI HP9 22 C5
s Cres HP9 23 E3
s Rd HP9 22 D5
CI HP13 20 C2
ts Ct HP16 8 B5

Burnham Av HP9 23 H5
Burnham CI,
  Bourne End SL8 25 B6
Burnham CI,
  High Wycombe HP12 18 D1
Burnham Rd HP14 11 G6
Burroughs Cres SL8 25 A5
Burrows CI HP10 17 G4
Burrows Ho HP13 15 E3
Burton La HP27 4 C2
Burtons La HP8 36 C4
Burtons Way HP8 37 C5
Bury Farm HP7 34 C5
Bury La HP5 32 C2
Buryfield La HP16 9 F2
Bushey CI HP12 19 E1
Buslins La HP5 30 A4
Butler Ct SL7 27 F5
Butlers CI HP6 34 B2
Butlers Court Rd HP23 23 E4
Butlers Ct HP13 20 D3
Butterfield HP10 25 E6
Butterly Rd HP14 6 D6
Byron CI SL7 27 F5
By-Wood End SL9 40 E1

C.R. Bates Ind Est HP14 6 C5
Cairnside HP13 20 C2
Caledon CI HP9 23 F2
Caledon Rd HP9 23 F2
California Cir HP11 19 H4
Calumet HP9 23 E2
Calverley Cres HP13 15 F4
Cambridge Cres HP13 20 C1
Cambridge Rd,
  Beaconsfield HP9 22 D3
Cambridge Rd,
  Marlow SL7 27 C6
Camden PI SL8 25 B7
Cameron Rd HP5 32 D1
Camp Rd SL9 41 B8
Campbell CI HP13 15 F6
Campbell Dr HP9 22 C3
Campbells Ride HP15 13 G5
Campion Rd HP15 12 D5
Candlemas La HP9 23 F3
Candlemas Mead HP9 23 F3
Candlemas Oaks HP9 23 F3
Candytuft Grn HP15 12 D6
Cane End HP27 4 A5
Cannon Mill Av HP5 33 E4
Cannon PI HP27 4 B3
Canterbury CI,
  Amersham HP7 35 F4
Canterbury CI,
  Princes Risborough HP27 4 B3
Capetown Cotts SL7 27 A6
Captain Cook CI HP8 38 C5
Captains CI HP5 13 F6
Carisbrooke Av HP12 18 B2
Carlton Ct HP27 4 B5
Carmel Ct SL7 27 A7
Caroline Ct SL7 27 D5
Carrington Av HP10 24 A2
Carrington PI HP15 13 F5
Carrington Rd HP12 19 E2
Carrington Way HP16 8 B4
Carrs Dr HP12 14 C6
Carter Walk HP10 17 F6
Carver Hill Rd HP11 19 F3
Cascadia CI HP11 21 F6
Castle Est HP12 18 D4
Castle Hill HP11 3 A6
Castle PI HP13 3 C4
Castle St HP13 3 B4
Castle View Gdns
HP12 19 E1
Castleton CI SL7 27 D6
Cater Rd HP14 28 C2
Catherine Ct HP12 18 B5
Catkin CI HP12 18 B5
Cavendish CI HP6 36 B4
Cavendish Rd HP5 33 E3
Cedar Av HP15 12 D6
Cedar CI HP5 31 F6
Cedar Cotts HP16 8 C4
Cedar Ct,
  High Wycombe HP13 3 D4
Cedar Ct, Marlow SL7 27 D6
Cedar Dr SL7 26 B1
Cedar Gro HP7 34 D4
Cedar Ridge HP6 29 B2
Cedar Ter HP11 15 F6
Cedars CI SL9 40 D1
Centenary Way HP6 35 F3

Central Park Bsns Centre
  HP13 3 A3
Centre Par HP27 4 C2
Centre Walk HP15 17 E3
Cestreham Cres HP5 31 E6
Chacombe PI HP9 28 C6
Chadwick St HP13 16 A4
Chairborough Rd
  HP12 18 D3
Chalfont Av HP6 36 D4
Chalfont Rd HP9 29 B4
Chalfont St Peter By-Pass
  SL9 40 D3
Chalfont Station Rd
  HP7 36 C4
Chalfont Way HP12 18 D5
Chalford Flats HP10 24 F3
Chalk Farm Rd HP14 6 B4
Chalk Hill HP5 30 C6
Chalk La HP6 29 A3
Chalklands SL8 25 A5
Chalkpit La SL7 27 A5
Chalkstream Way
  HP10 24 E3
Challener Rd HP12 18 C5
Chancery Ct HP12 19 E3
Chandos CI HP6 36 B3
Channer Dr HP10 17 E5
Chapel End SL9 40 B4
Chapel Hill HP27 5 E3
Chapel La,
  Naphill HP14 10 D5
Chapel La,
  West Wycombe HP12 14 C6
Chapel Rd HP10 24 A2
Chapel St,
  High Wycombe HP13 15 E3
Chapel St,
  Marlow SL7 27 D6
Chapman La,
  Bourne End SL8 25 A5
Chapman La,
  Flackwell Heath HP10 24 B3
Chapmans Cres HP5 30 B6
Charlotte Way SL7 27 D6
Charnwood CI HP10 20 D3
Charsley CI HP6 36 B3
Charter Dr HP6 35 F3
Chartridge Ho HP13 20 C2
Chartridge La HP5 30 A5
Chartwell Gate HP9 23 E3
Chenies Av HP6 36 C4
Chenies Par HP7 36 C4
Chepping CI HP10 17 E4
Chequers Cotts HP14 28 B1
Chequers Dr HP16 8 A3
Chequers Hill HP7 34 D5
Chequers La HP16 8 B3
Chequers Par HP16 8 A3
Cherry Acre SL9 39 E6
Cherry CI,
  Great Missenden HP16 8 C4
Cherry CI,
  High Wycombe HP10 24 B3
Cherry Crnr HP10 24 B1
Cherry Dr HP9 22 C1
Cherry Gro HP15 13 G6
Cherry La HP7 34 A6
Cherry Orch HP6 35 F2
Cherry Orchard Ct
  HP13 20 B2
Cherry Rise,
  Chalfont St Giles HP8 38 E3
Cherry Rise,
  High Wycombe HP10 24 C3
Cherry St HP13 21 E4
Cherry Tree CI,
  Great Kingshill HP15 12 B2
Cherry Tree CI,
  Hughenden Valley HP14 11 G4
Cherry Tree CI, Princes
  Risborough HP27 5 F3
Cherry Tree La HP16 7 C3
Cherry Tree Rd HP9 22 B4
Cherry Tree Walk HP5 31 E5
Cherry Tree Way HP10 17 G4
Cherry Way HP15 13 E6
Cherrycroft Dr HP14 11 E6
Cherrytree La SL8 40 B4
Cherrywood CI HP9 29 B4
Cherrywood Gdns
  HP10 24 B2
Cherwell Rd SL8 25 B5

Chesham Cottage
  Hospital HP5 32 D3
Chesham La SL9 39 F5
Chesham Rd,
  Amersham HP6 34 D1
Chesham Rd,
  Chesham HP5 30 A1
Chesham Rd,
  Great Missenden HP16 9 G3
Chess CI HP5 36 C1
Chessbury CI HP5 32 B3
Chessbury Rd HP5 32 B3
Chessfield Pk HP6 36 D4
Chessmount Rise HP5 33 E4
Chesterton CI HP5 30 C6
Chesterton Ct HP11 3 A5
Chesterton Grn HP9 23 F3
Chestnut Av,
  Chesham HP5 31 F6
Chestnut Av,
  High Wycombe HP11 20 B3
Chestnut CI,
  Amersham HP6 35 E2
Chestnut CI,
  Gerrards Cross SL9 40 D3
Chestnut CI,
  Princes Risborough HP27 4 C2
Chestnut Ct HP6 35 E1
Chestnut La,
  Amersham HP6 35 E1
Chestnut La,
  High Wycombe HP15 17 E1
Chestnut Rd,
  Beaconsfield HP9 22 C4
Chestnut Rd,
  Princes Risborough HP27 4 C5
Chestnut Walk SL9 40 D3
Cheviot CI HP13 15 E5
Cheyne CI HP6 32 D6
Cheyne Walk HP5 32 D1
Chichester CI HP13 20 B2
Chichester Ho HP12 19 E3
Chichester Row HP6 35 E2
Chilcote La HP7 36 A4
Chiltern Av,
  Amersham HP6 34 D3
Chiltern Av,
  High Wycombe HP12 18 D3
Chiltern CI HP27 4 B5
Chiltern Commercial Centre
  HP5 30 C6
Chiltern Ct,
  Chesham HP5 30 C6
Chiltern Ct,
  High Wycombe HP12 19 E1
Chiltern Ct,
  Loudwater HP10 21 G6
Chiltern Grn HP10 24 A2
Chiltern Heights,
  Amersham HP7 35 H4
Chiltern Heights,
  High Wycombe HP11 3 A6
Chiltern Hill SL9 40 C3
Chiltern Hills Rd HP9 22 D3
Chiltern Manor Pk
  HP16 9 E2
Chiltern Par HP6 34 D2
Chiltern Rd,
  Amersham HP6 32 C6
Chiltern Rd, Great
  Missenden HP16 7 D4
Chiltern Rd,
  Marlow SL7 27 B6
Chiltern Ridge HP14 6 A5
Chiltern Vw HP14 6 D1
Chilterns CI HP10 24 B2
Chilterns Pk SL8 25 B5
Chilton CI,
  Holmer Green HP15 13 G4
Chilton CI,
  Tylers Green HP5 30 D5
Chimney La HP10 24 F2
Chinnor Rd HP14 6 A2
Chippendale CI HP16 8 B5
Chipstead SL9 40 A4
Christies CI HP13 3 C3
Christopher CI HP10 10 D5
Church Cotts HP14 6 A2
Church Ct HP13 16 B4
Church Farm Cotts
  HP16 7 A2

Church Gro HP6 36 D4
Church La,
  Bedlow Ridge HP14 6 A3
Church La,
  Chalfont St Peter SL9 40 C3
Church La,
  Great Missenden
  HP16 9 G3
Church La,
  Lacey Green HP27 5 B3
Church La,
  Naphill HP14 11 F6
Church La,
  Princes Risborough
  HP27 4 B4
Church La,
  Totteridge HP15 15 H2
Church La,
  West Wycombe HP14 14 A4
Church Path,
  Great Missenden
  HP16 8 C5
Church Path,
  High Wycombe HP14 6 B4
Church Rd,
  Lane End HP14 28 B3
Church Rd,
  Bourne End SL8 25 D8
Church Rd,
  Lane End HP14 28 B3
Church Rd, Penn HP10 17 F5
Church Rd,
  Seer Green HP9 29 B4
Church Sq HP11 3 B4
Church St,
  Amersham HP7 34 C5
Church St,
  Chesham HP5 32 C3
Church St,
  Great Missenden HP16 9 F3
Church St,
  High Wycombe HP11 3 B4
Church St, Princes
  Risborough HP27 4 B4
Church St,
  Stokenchurch HP14 6 B4
Churchfield Rd SL9 40 C3
Churchill CI HP10 24 C3
Churchill Dr,
  Beaconsfield HP9 28 C6
Churchill Dr,
  Marlow SL7 26 E4
Churchside HP15 13 G4
Clappins La HP14 10 C4
Clapton App HP10 24 D1
Clare Pk HP7 35 E5
Clare Rd HP16 8 A4
Claremont Gdns SL7 27 D6
Claremont Rd SL7 27 D6
Clarence Ct HP13 3 D3
Clarendon Rd,
  Great Missenden
  HP16 8 A3
Clarendon Rd,
  High Wycombe HP13 20 C2
Clarke Dr HP13 21 E2
Clarks Cotts HP16 8 A2
Clauds CI HP15 17 E1
Clay Acre HP5 32 D1
Clay CI HP10 24 B2
Clay La SL7 18 A6
Clay Lane Farm Cotts
  SL7 18 B6
Clay St HP9 28 B4
Claydon Ct HP12 19 E4
Claydon End SL9 41 D5
Claydon La SL9 41 D5
Clayfields HP10 17 F4
Clayhill SL7 18 B6
Claymoor SL7 18 A6
Clayton Walk HP7 36 B4
Claytons Mdw SL8 25 B7
Clearbrook CI HP13 21 F3
Cleland Rd SL9 41 C5
Clementi Av HP15 13 G5
Cleveland CI HP10 24 F2
Clifford Rd HP27 4 B5
Cliffords Way SL8 25 B5
Clifton CI HP11 19 F4
Clifton Lawns HP6 32 C6
Clifton PI SL8 25 D7
Clifton Rd HP6 32 C5
Cliveden Office Village
  HP12 19 E4
Coach Ride SL7 27 C4
Coat Wicks HP9 29 A5
Coaters La HP10 24 E2

Coates La HP13 15 E3
Cock La HP13 20 D3
Cockpit Cl HP15 12 C3
Cockpit Cotts HP15 12 B3
Cockpit Rd HP15 12 B4
Codmore Cres HP5 33 E1
Codmore Wood Rd
HP5 36 D1
Coffins Ho HP11 3 A4
Cokes Farm La HP8 37 A4
Cokes La HP8 37 A7
Colborne Rd HP13 16 B6
Coleheath Bottom HP27 5 F3
Colliers Row HP14 6 B2
Collings Walk HP16 8 B5
Collingwood Cl HP13 21 E2
Collyer Rd HP14 6 C5
Colne Rd HP13 20 D1
Colston Ct SL9 41 D8
Columbine Rd HP15 12 D5
Colville Cl HP6 9 F3
Colville Rd HP11 19 F1
Combe Rise HP12 18 C1
Comino La SL8 25 B6
Commercial Sq HP11 19 F1
Common Rd,
Flackwell Heath HP10 24 B1
Common Rd,
Great Kingshill HP15 12 B3
Common Wood La
HP10 17 G5
Commonside HP13 15 E3
Conegra Ct HP13 3 D4
Conegra Rd HP13 3 D4
Conifer Rise HP12 19 E2
Coningsby Ct HP13 3 C1
Coningsby Rd HP13 3 C1
Conniston Cl SL7 27 B6
Conway Cl HP10 21 G6
Cookham Ct HP6 35 F3
Cooks Cl SL9 40 C1
Coombe Gdns HP14 11 G6
Coombe La HP14 11 H6
Coopers Rise HP13 20 B2
Copes Rd HP15 12 C3
Copes Shroves HP15 12 D6
Copners Dr HP15 13 F6
Copners Way HP15 13 F6
Copper Ridge SL9 40 E1
Copperfields,
Beaconsfield HP9 28 D6
Copperfields,
High Wycombe HP14 14 C5
Copperkins Gro HP6 34 C1
Copperkins La HP6 29 C3
Coppice Farm Rd HP10 17 F3
Copse Cl SL7 27 B6
Copse La HP9 29 C6
Copse Way HP5 30 C3
Copthall Cl SL9 40 D2
Copthall Corner SL9 40 D2
Copthall La SL9 40 D2
Copyground Ct HP12 19 E1
Copyground La HP12 15 E6
Cordons SL9 40 C3
Cores End Rd SL8 25 B6
Corinium Ind Est HP6 35 F3
Cornel Cl HP15 17 E3
Cornerways HP27 5 F3
Coronation Cres HP14 28 C2
Coronation Rd HP12 18 D4
Corporation St HP11 3 C5
Costers Cotts SL8 25 C8
Cotswold Way HP13 15 E5
CottaGe Farm Way
HP27 5 F3
Coulson St HP11 3 C5
Court Cl,
High Wycombe HP13 14 D4
Court Cl,
Princes Risborough
HP27 4 A4
Court Lawns HP10 17 G5
Court Rd HP14 6 B4
Courtmoor Cl HP27 4 C2
Courtyard Cl HP6 34 D3
Cowal Cl HP15 12 C2
Cowper Rd HP5 30 C6
Cowslip Rd HP15 12 D5
Coxfield Cl HP14 6 C4
Crab Tree Cl HP9 22 C4
Crabbe Cres HP5 31 E6
Craigleith Ct HP13 23 E3
Crendon St HP11 3 C5
Cressex Bsns Pk HP12 18 D3
Cressex Enterprise Centre
HP12 19 E2

Cressex Rd HP12 18 B5
Cressington Ct SL8 25 A5
Cressington Pl SL8 25 A5
Cresswell Rd HP5 33 E5
Cresswell Way HP15 13 G5
Crest Rd HP11 18 D5
Cricket Ground HP14 6 B4
Cricket Hill SL8 25 C8
Crispin Cl HP9 23 E1
Crispin Way HP11 19 G4
Criss Gro SL9 40 B4
Crocketts La HP16 7 C3
Croft Rd SL9 40 C4
Croftwood HP13 16 D6
Crompton Hall SL9 41 D7
Cromwell Cl HP8 38 D4
Cromwell Gdns SL7 27 D4
Cromwell Ho HP5 32 C1
Cromwell Rd, High
Wycombe HP13 20 C3
Cromwell Rd,
Marlow SL7 27 D6
Crosby Cl HP9 23 G5
Crosby Ho SL8 25 B6
Cross Bed Villas HP5 33 F6
Cross Ct HP13 14 D4
Cross La HP9 23 G6
Cross Lanes SL9 40 D1
Cross Mdw HP5 30 A6
Cross Rd HP12 18 D1
Crossfield Rd HP27 4 C3
Crossleys HP8 38 D5
Crossway HP5 33 E1
Crossways,
Beaconsfield HP9 23 G4
Crossways,
High Wycombe HP12 18 C4
Crowbrook Rd HP27 4 C2
Crown Bsns Est HP5 30 D6
Crown Cotts HP27 5 B3
Crown La,
High Wycombe HP11 3 B5
Crown La,
Marlow SL7 27 D6
Crown Rd SL7 27 C6
Crusader Est HP12 18 D3
Crutches La HP9 29 D5
Cryers Hill La HP15 12 B5
Cryers Hill Rd HP15 11 H6
Cullyn Rd HP12 18 C5
Culvers Cft HP9 29 B5
Culverton Hill HP27 4 B5
Culverton La HP27 4 B6
Cumberland Cl HP7 36 A4
Cumbrian Way HP13 15 F5
Curlew Cl HP13 14 C4
Curtis Cotts HP5 31 G1
Curzon Av,
Beaconsfield HP9 23 E1
Curzon Av,
High Wycombe HP15 17 F4
Curzon Cl HP15 17 F3
Curzon Gate Ct HP14 6 C4
Cypress Walk HP15 17 F3

Dairymede HP27 5 F3
Daisy Cotts HP14 28 B3
Dandridge Dr SL8 25 C6
Darlington Cl HP6 35 E3
Darvell Dr HP5 30 B5
Darvills Mdw HP15 13 F4
Dashfield Gro HP15 12 C4
Dashwood Av HP12 14 D6
Davenies Mews HP9 23 F3
Davenport Rd HP12 18 C5
Davidge Pl HP9 28 B6
Davies Way HP10 24 D1
Davis Cl SL7 27 E7
Dawes Cl HP5 32 B3
Daws Hill La HP11 19 G3
Daws Lea HP11 19 G4
Daywise Ct HP12 18 D4
De Havilland Dr HP15 16 C3
De Pirenore HP15 16 C4
Deacon Cl HP12 18 C4
Deadhearn La HP8 39 E2
Dean Cl HP12 19 F2
Dean Way,
Chalfont St Giles
HP8 38 B5
Dean Way,
High Wycombe HP15 13 F6
Dean Wood Rd HP9 29 B6
Deanacre Cl SL9 40 C1
Deancroft Rd SL9 40 D1
Deanfield HP14 6 B1

Deanfield Cl,
High Wycombe HP14 6 D2
Deanfield Cl,
Marlow SL7 27 C5
Deanfield Cotts HP14 11 F2
Deangarden Rise HP11 20 C3
Deans Cl HP6 35 F2
Deansway HP5 30 C6
Dedmere Ct SL7 27 E6
Dedmere Rd SL7 27 E6
Dedmere Rise SL7 27 E6
Deeds Gro HP12 19 E1
Deep Acres HP6 34 B1
Deep Mill La HP16 13 G1
Deer Mead HP16 9 F6
Deer Park Walk HP5 31 F5
Dell Fld HP14 6 D5
Dell Fld HP14 8 B5
Delmeade Rd HP5 32 B3
Dene Cotts HP14 10 C4
Dene Wood HP13 16 C6
Denham La SL9 40 D1
Denham Rd HP14 28 C1
Denham Walk SL9 40 D2
Denmark St HP11 3 A4
Denton Cl SL7 27 E5
Derehams Av HP10 21 G5
Derehams La HP10 21 G6
Derwent Cl HP7 36 A4
Desborough Av HP11 19 F4
Desborough Ho HP13 3 D4
Desborough Ind Pk
HP12 15 E6
Desborough Park Rd
HP12 15 E6
Desborough Rd HP11 3 A4
Desborough St HP11 15 F6
Devonshire Av HP6 34 C2
Devonshire Ct HP11 34 C1
Dilwyns Ct HP12 15 E6
Disraeli Cres HP13 15 F4
Disraeli Pk HP9 23 E1
Dodds La HP8 38 B3
Doggetts Wood Cl
HP8 37 B6
Doggetts Wood La
HP8 37 B6
Dolphin Ct HP11 21 E5
Donkey La SL8 25 A6
Donnay Cl SL9 41 B8
Donnybrook Ho HP13 3 D4
Dorchester Rd HP14 6 D1
Dormer La HP15 13 E5
Dorney End HP5 32 A1
Douglas Ct SL7 27 F5
Dove Ct HP9 23 E3
Dovecot Rd HP13 3 A3
Dovecote Cl HP27 4 C2
Dovetail Cl HP12 14 D6
Dower Cl HP9 22 D1
Downley Rd HP14 10 D6
Downs Pk HP11 15 E4
Drake Cl HP11 21 E5
Drakes Rd HP7 35 E4
Dresser Rd HP16 8 B4
Drews Pk HP9 28 B5
Drovers Way HP9 29 A5
Drydell Cotts HP5 32 B3
Drydell La HP5 32 A2
Du Pre Walk HP10 25 D6
Duke St,
High Wycombe HP13 3 D5
Duke St,
Princes Risborough
HP27 4 B4
Dukes Mdw Ind Est
SL8 25 C6
Dukes Pl SL7 27 C6
Duncan Lock Ho HP9 23 G3
Duncombe Cl HP6 35 F3
Dunkeld Ho HP11 21 E4
Dunsmore Av HP27 4 C2
Dunsmore Ride HP27 4 C2
Dunstable Ho SL7 27 F6
Dunwood Rise HP13 15 H5
Durley Hollow HP13 15 H5
Durrants Path HP5 30 C4

Eagle Cl HP6 35 G2
Eagle Ct HP6 35 G2
Earl Cl HP13 15 G5
Earl Howe Rd HP15 13 G5
East Common SL9 41 D8
East Dr HP13 16 C6

East Richardson St
HP11 19 F1
East Ridge SL8 25 C5
East St HP5 32 C2
East Way HP9 22 B5
Eastergate HP9 22 D1
Eastern Dene HP15 17 E1
Eastern Dr SL8 25 D7
Eastfield Rd HP27 4 C4
Eastlands HP27 5 B2
Easton St HP11 3 C5
Easton Ter HP13 3 D5
Eastwood Ct SL7 27 E5
Eastwood Rd HP14 6 D6
Eaton Av HP12 14 D6
Eaton Pl HP12 14 D6
Ebenezer Ho HP10 21 G6
Edgar Wallace Pl SL8 24 B4
Edgecote Ho HP13 3 C3
Edgewood HP11 20 B3
Edinburgh Rd SL7 27 E5
Edmonds Rd HP14 28 C2
Edmund Ct HP9 22 C5
Edmunds Cl HP12 18 C2
Edmunds Gdns HP12 18 C2
Edwin Allman Pl HP15 16 C3
Eghams Cl HP9 22 D1
Eghams Ct SL8 25 D6
Eghams Grn SL8 25 B6
Eghams Wood Rd
HP9 22 D1
Elder Cl HP11 21 F5
Elder Way HP15 17 E3
Eleanor Rd SL9 40 B3
Elgiva La HP5 32 C2
Eliot Dr SL7 26 E4
Elizabeth Av HP6 36 B3
Elizabeth Ct HP13 20 A2
Elizabeth Rd, High
Wycombe HP14 6 C6
Elizabeth Rd,
Marlow SL7 27 D5
Ellis Av SL9 40 D3
Ellis Way HP14 28 C3
Ellsworth Rd HP11 19 F3
Ellwood Ho SL9 40 C3
Ellwood Rd HP9 22 C4
Ellwood Rise HP8 38 D3
Elm Cl,
Amersham HP6 34 D3
Elm Cl,
High Wycombe HP15 17 E2
Elm Cotts HP10 22 A5
Elm La SL8 25 A5
Elm Rd, Booker HP12 18 C4
Elm Rd,
Princes Risborough
HP27 4 C4
Elm Tree Hill HP5 32 C1
Elmdale Gdns HP27 4 B4
Elmhurst HP16 9 F2
Elmhurst Cl HP13 16 B4
Elms Dr SL8 25 C6
Elms Rd SL9 40 C2
Elmshott Cl HP10 17 E4
Elmtree Cl HP16 9 F2
Elmtree Grn HP16 9 F2
Elora Rd HP13 16 B6
Elwes Rd HP14 28 C2
Ely Cl HP7 35 F4
Ely Ho,
Stokenchurch HP14 6 B4
Ely Ho,
Totteridge HP13 16 D6
Ercolani Av HP13 20 B2
Eskdale Av HP5 32 D1
Eskdale Lodge HP6 34 D2
Essex Rd HP5 30 D6
Estcourt Dr HP5 12 C6
Ethorpe Cl SL9 41 D7
Ethorpe Cres SL9 41 D7
Eton Pl SL7 27 C6
Eunice Gro HP5 33 E3
Evenlode Rd SL8 25 B5
Everest Cl HP13 20 B1
Everest Rd HP13 20 B1

Factory Yd HP9 23 F5
Fair Acres HP16 8 B4
Fair Leas HP5 30 B6
Fair Ridge HP11 19 F4
Fairfax Mews HP7 34 B5
Fairfield Cl SL8 25 A5
Fairfields HP15 12 C3

Fairhaven SL9 40 C7
Fairview Ind Est,
Amersham HP6
Fairview Ind Est,
High Wycombe HP11
Fairview La HP10
Fairway HP27
Faithorn Cl HP15
Falcon Rise HP12 4 C4
Falcons Cft HP10
Farm Cl,
Amersham HP6
Farm Cl,
High Wycombe HP13
Farm Gro HP9
Farm La HP9
Farm Rd SL8
Farmers Way HP10
Farndale Gdns HP15
Fassetts Rd HP10
Faulkner Way HP13
Featherbed La HP15
Fennels Farm Rd HP10
Fennels Rd HP11
Fennels Way HP10
Fern Walk HP15
Ferndale Cl HP14
Fernhurst Cl HP9
Fernie Flds HP12
Fernlea Cl HP10
Fernleigh Ct SL8
Fernside,
Great Kingshill HP15
Fernside,
Widmer End HP15
Ferrington Cl SL9
Ferry La SL8
Field Cl HP5
Field Rd HP12
Fieldhead Gdns SL8
Fieldhouse Ind Est
SL7
Fieldhouse La SL7
Fieldhouse Way SL7
Fieldway,
Amersham HP7
Fieldway,
Gerrards Cross SL9
Fifth St HP11
Finch End HP10
Finch La,
Amersham HP7
Finch La,
Beaconsfield HP9
Finings Rd HP14
Fir Tree Cotts HP14
Firs Cl,
Lane End HP14
Firs Cl,
Totteridge HP13
Firs Cl,
Tylers Green HP15
Firs Ct HP6
Firs End SL9
Firs Rise HP16
Firs View Rd HP15
Firs Walk HP15
First Av,
Amersham HP7
First Av, Marlow SL7
First St HP11
Firview Cl SL7
Fishermans Retreat
SL8
Fishermans Way SL8
Fitzgeralds Way HP12
Five Acre Wood HP12
Five Acres,
Chesham HP5
Five Acres,
High Wycombe HP10
Flaunden Bottom HP5
Fleet Cl HP14
Fleetwood Cl HP8
Fleming Way HP12
Flint Way HP16
Flitcroft Lea HP13
Florida St HP11
Flowers Bottom La
HP27
Foley Cl HP9
Folio Ho HP10
Ford St HP11
Ford Way HP13
Fords Cl HP14
Forelands Way HP5

...ottom La,
...onsfield HP9 23 G1
...onsfield La,
...Green HP9 29 A5
...ield HP16 9 G6
...ield Dr HP6 34 C3
...ield Rd HP5 30 B5
...and Way HP12 18 D3
...iew HP9 22 B5
...vick Rd HP27 4 A2
...ood La HP7 35 E4
...ey Hill HP27 5 A2
...Mill Ct HP5 32 D3
...ne Cl HP13 16 C6
...es La HP14 11 E5
...ams Rd HP7 36 B4
...ams Wood La 37 C5
...End SL9 40 B3
...Mead SL9 40 B3
...Rd SL9 40 B3
...on Cl HP11 20 A4
...Church St HP14 6 C4
...Dr HP9 23 E1
...Furney Cl HP13 16 B6
...Hammersley La 21 E4
Icknield Way 4 A1
...Lodge La HP15 13 E6
...Pound La SL7 27 C8
...Rd,
...ards Cross SL9 40 C4
...Rd, Princes
...borough HP27 5 A3
...Ridge SL8 25 B6
...Riding HP9 22 C4
...Cl HP14 6 A4
...ield Cl HP15 17 E3
...ield Way HP15 17 E3
...nds Cres HP15 12 B2
...des Av HP5 32 B1
...Rd HP13 3 D3
...w Mews HP11 21 E4
...ne La HP5 31 F5
...ne Rd HP5 31 F5
...een Rd HP5 33 E1
...urst Cl HP13 14 D4
...urst Rd HP5 30 C5
...n Cl HP16 8 B3
...n Gdns HP13 16 C6
...d Par HP15 13 G5
...d Rd HP5 30 D5
...onald Cl HP6 32 D6
...nnan Pl HP12 18 D3
...ey Cl HP6 35 E1
...olia Dene HP5 16 C3
...olia Way HP10 24 E2
...e Cl HP10 24 A1
...e La,
...well Heath 24 A1
...e La,
...water HP13 21 F5
...Dr SL9 41 B7
...Rd,
...Green HP27 5 A2
...Rd,
...ill HP14 10 D5
...Rd,
...rs Ash HP14 10 B2
...nd Dr HP13 3 C1
...n Cl HP6 35 F3
...Cl HP14 6 C4
...Dr HP9 22 D2
...d Ho HP11 20 A2
...d Pl HP11 21 E5
...ers Well Rd HP13 3 C3
...ouse Sq,
...onsfield HP9 23 G5
...ouse Sq,
...es Risborough 4 B4
...ouse Way SL7 27 C7
...ans La SL9 41 B5
...lia HP13 15 E5
...ville Rd HP16 8 A2
...Cl HP10 17 E3
...Cotts HP16 7 B2
...Court Yd HP13 3 B1
...Cres HP9 29 B4
...Ct SL7 27 C5
...Dr HP6 34 C1
...Farm Way HP9 29 B5
...Gdns,
...Wycombe HP13 15 H5

Manor Gdns,
  Wooburn HP10 24 F4
Manor Park Av HP27 4 A5
Manor Rd,
  Beaconsfield HP9 29 B4
Manor Rd,
  Chesham HP5 30 D6
Manor Rd,
  High Wycombe HP15 16 D3
Manor Rd, Princes
  Risborough HP27 4 A5
Manor Vw HP15 17 E4
Manor Way HP5 33 E1
Maple Cl,
  Cressex HP12 18 D3
Maple Cl,
  Hazlemere HP15 17 E3
Maple Cl HP5 32 C1
Maple Rise SL7 27 D5
Maplefield La HP8 37 B5
Maplewood Gdns HP9 22 C4
Marchant Ct SL7 27 F5
Marcourt Rd HP14 6 C6
Marefield Rd SL7 27 C6
Margaret Cotts HP14 11 E2
Marigold Walk HP15 12 D6
Mark Dr SL9 39 E6
Market Par HP15 16 D2
Market Pl SL9 40 C3
Market Sq,
  Amersham HP7 34 C5
Market Sq,
  Chesham HP5 32 C2
Market Sq,
  Marlow SL7 27 C6
Market Sq, Princes
  Risborough HP27 4 B4
Marlborough Ind Est
  HP11 15 F6
Marlin Ct SL7 27 F7
Marlow Bottom SL7 26 B1
Marlow Bridge La SL7 27 D7
Marlow By-Pass SL7 26 E1
Marlow Ct HP6 35 F3
Marlow Hill HP11 3 B6
Marlow Hospital
  SL7 27 D6
Marlow Mill SL7 27 E7
Marlow Pk SL7 27 E6
Marlow Rd,
  Bourne End SL8 25 A5
Marlow Rd,
  High Wycombe HP11 19 E5
Marlow Rd,
  Lane End HP14 28 C3
Marlow Rd,
  Marlow SL7 26 A1
Marlow Rd,
  Stokenchurch HP14 6 C5
Marsh Ct HP11 20 D3
Marsham La SL9 41 D8
Marsham Lodge SL9 41 D8
Marsham Way SL9 41 D7
Marston Cl HP5 30 B4
Martin Dell Cotts HP16 7 C3
Martinsend La HP16 7 C3
Martyrs Ct HP7 34 D4
Marygold Walk HP6 36 B4
Marys Mead HP15 16 D1
Masefield Cl HP5 30 C5
Masons Cl HP16 8 B4
Maude Cl HP9 23 H4
Maude Rd HP9 23 H4
Maurice Mount HP15 12 D6
Maxwell Dr HP15 17 E1
Maxwell Rd HP9 23 F3
May Tree Cl SL7 26 B2
Maybrook Gdns HP13 3 D2
Maybush Gdns HP15 8 B3
Mayfield Av SL9 41 C6
Mayfield Rd HP10 24 F3
Mayflower Way HP9 22 B5
Mayhall La HP6 32 C6
Mayhew Cres HP13 16 B6
Mead Acre HP27 4 B2
Mead Cl, Marlow SL7 27 E5
Mead Cl,
  Princes Risborough
  HP27 4 C2
Mead Pk HP15 13 F4
Mead Platt HP14 6 B4
Mead St HP13 21 E4
Mead Way HP11 20 D4
Meades La HP5 32 C3
Meadow Bank SL8 25 B6
Meadow Cl,
  Chesham HP5 30 B3

Meadow Cl,
  High Wycombe HP11 20 D4
Meadow Cl,
  Marlow SL7 27 E7
Meadow Cotts,
  Beaconsfield HP9 23 F4
Meadow Cotts,
  Great Missenden
  HP16 13 F1
Meadow Dr HP6 35 E2
Meadow Gate HP16 12 A1
Meadow La HP9 23 G3
Meadow Rise HP27 5 B3
Meadow Vw,
  Chalfont St Giles HP8 38 B5
Meadow Vw,
  Marlow SL7 26 D2
Meadow Walk,
  Bourne End SL8 25 B5
Meadow Walk,
  High Wycombe HP10 17 G5
Meadow Way HP6 29 B2
Meadowcroft SL9 40 C4
Meadowside HP9 29 D6
Meare Est HP10 24 E2
Meavy Cl HP13 21 F4
Melbourne Rd HP13 20 D1
Melissa Ct HP13 20 B2
Melrose Ct HP13 15 H5
Mendip Way HP13 15 F5
Mendy St HP11 3 A4
Mentmore Cl HP12 18 C2
Mentmore Rd HP12 18 C2
Mere Cl HP13 17 E3
Mere Court Cl SL7 27 E6
Mere Pk SL7 27 E6
Merlewood Cl HP11 19 H4
Merrydown HP13 15 E5
Merton Rd HP27 4 B5
Micholls Av SL9 39 F6
Micklefield Rd HP13 16 D6
Mid Cross La SL9 40 D1
Middle Cl HP6 35 F2
Middle Dr HP9 28 D6
Middle Mdw HP8 38 D5
Middlebrook Rd HP13 15 E5
Midsummer Ct HP15 17 E2
Miersfield HP13 18 D5
Mile Elm SL7 27 F5
Milestone Cl HP14 6 C4
Mill Cl HP5 33 F5
Mill Cotts,
  Wooburn HP10 24 E2
Mill Cotts,
  Wooburn Green
  HP10 25 E5
Mill End Rd HP14 14 C6
Mill Ho SL8 25 B8
Mill La,
  Amersham HP7 34 B4
Mill La,
  Beaconsfield HP9 23 F4
Mill La,
  Chalfont St Giles HP8 38 B4
Mill La,
  Gerrards Cross SL9 41 D8
Mill La,
  Great Missenden
  HP16 9 G2
Mill La,
  High Wycombe HP14 6 A4
Mill La,
  Princes Risborough
  HP27 4 A1
Mill Rd,
  High Wycombe HP14 6 A5
Mill Rd, Marlow SL7 27 D7
Mill Stream Ct HP27 4 A6
Millbank SL7 27 E7
Millboard Rd SL8 25 C7
Millbrook Cl HP12 14 D5
Milldun Way HP12 19 E2
Miller Pl SL9 41 C7
Millers Cres HP11 20 D3
Millfields HP5 32 D4
Millgate HP11 20 D3
Millshot Dr HP7 34 D5
Millside,
  Bourne End SL8 25 C6
Millside,
  Riversdale SL8 25 B8
Millstream Ho SL8 25 B8
Millstream Way HP10 24 E1
Milton Av SL9 41 B6
Milton Flds HP8 38 C4
Milton Gdns HP27 4 A5
Milton Hill HP8 38 C4

Milton Lawns HP6 35 E1
Milton Rd HP5 30 C6
Mineral La HP5 32 C3
Minerva Way HP9 23 G4
Misbourne Av,
  Gerrards Cross SL9 40 C1
Misbourne Av, High
  Wycombe HP13 20 D2
Misbourne Cl SL9 40 C1
Misbourne Dr HP16 9 F3
Misbourne Ho HP8 38 C2
Misbourne Vale SL9 39 E6
Missenden Mews HP16 9 F2
Missenden Rd,
  Chesham HP5 32 A3
Missenden Rd,
  Great Missenden
  HP16 12 B1
Mitchell Ho HP11 20 B2
Mitchell Walk HP6 35 E3
Moat Cl HP16 8 B3
Moat Dr HP16 8 B3
Moat La HP16 8 B2
Mole Run HP13 14 D4
Monks Hollow SL7 26 D3
Monkton Way HP27 5 F3
Montford Mews HP15 16 C4
Monument La SL9 40 D1
Moonstone Ct HP13 14 D6
Moor La HP13 14 D3
Moor Rd HP5 32 C3
Moorside HP10 24 E2
Moreland Dr SL9 41 D8
Morris Cl SL9 40 E3
Morris Mews HP11 21 E5
Mortens Wood HP7 35 E5
Moseley Rd HP14 10 C5
Moses Plat La HP27 5 E3
Moss Ct HP9 29 B5
Mossway HP9 22 D1
Mount Cl HP12 19 E2
Mount Nugent HP5 30 B2
Mount Pleasant HP14 28 C1
Mount Pleasant Cotts
  SL8 25 B6
Mount Way HP27 4 A4
Mountain Ash SL7 26 C2
Moyleen Rise SL7 27 B7
Mulberry Cl,
  Amersham HP7 35 G4
Mulberry Cl,
  High Wycombe HP12 18 D2
Mulberry Ct,
  Beaconsfield HP9 23 G5
Mulberry Ct,
  High Wycombe HP15 13 G5
Munces Rd SL7 26 D3
Mundaydean La SL7 27 A5
Musgrave Walk HP14 6 C4
Mylne Ct HP13 15 G6
Mynchen Cl HP9 28 C5
Mynchen End HP9 28 C5
Mynchen Rd HP9 28 C6

Nags Head La HP16 9 E5
Nairdwood Cl HP16 8 D5
Nairdwood La HP16 8 D5
Nairdwood Way HP16 8 D5
Nalders Rd HP6 31 E6
Nancy Hall Ct HP12 18 D4
Narcot La HP8 38 B5
Narcot Rd HP8 38 B5
Narcot Way HP8 38 B5
Narrow La HP13 15 E3
Nash Ho,
  Amersham HP7 35 G4
Nash Ho,
  High Wycombe HP11 20 B2
Nash Pl HP10 17 F5
Nashleigh Ct HP5 31 E6
Nashleigh Hill HP5 31 E5
Natwoke Cl HP9 28 C6
Neale Cl HP12 18 D5
Needham Ct HP11 19 F1
Nelson Cl HP13 20 C3
Nelson Ct HP13 20 C3
Netherwood Rd HP9 28 D6
New Chilterns HP7 35 F4
New Ct,
  High Wycombe HP13 20 A2
New Ct, Marlow SL7 27 D6
New Dr HP13 16 B6
New Pond Rd HP15 13 G4
New Rd,
  Amersham HP6 35 F2
New Rd, Booker HP12 18 C1

New Rd,
  Bourne End SL8 25 B6
New Rd,
  Chalfont St Giles HP8 37 E6
New Rd,
  Great Kingshill HP15 12 A3
New Rd,
  Great Missenden
  HP16 9 G5
New Rd,
  Lacey Green HP27 5 C4
New Rd,
  Lane End HP14 28 A1
New Rd, Marlow SL7 26 C2
New Rd, Penn HP10 17 F5
New Rd,
  Prestwood HP16 8 C3
New Rd,
  Princes Risborough
  HP27 4 B4
New Rd,
  Stokenchurch HP14 6 D6
New Rd,
  Walters Ash HP27 10 A1
New Road Cl HP12 18 C2
New Road Gdns HP12 18 C2
Newbarn La HP9 38 A6
Newfield Gdns SL7 27 E5
Newfield Rd SL7 27 E6
Newfield Way SL7 27 E6
Newland St HP11 3 A5
Newmans Row HP12 19 E3
Newmer Rd HP12 18 B5
Newtown Rd SL7 27 E5
Nicholas Gdns HP13 16 B6
Nickson Ct HP15 16 D2
Nicol Cl SL8 40 B3
Nicol End SL9 40 A3
Nicol Rd SL9 40 A3
Nightingale Cl HP15 13 E6
Nightingale Rd HP5 30 D6
Nightingales Ct HP8 36 C4
Nightingales La, Chalfont St
  Giles HP8 39 E1
Nightingales La, Little
  Chalfont HP8 37 B6
Ninnings Rd SL9 40 E2
Ninnings Way SL9 40 D2
Niplands Cotts HP10 25 E7
Norgrove Pk SL9 41 C6
Norjo-An Villas HP5 32 D4
Norland Dr HP10 24 C2
Normans Ct HP13 20 D2
North Dr,
  Beaconsfield HP9 22 C5
North Dr,
  High Wycombe HP13 16 B5
North Links Rd HP10 24 B1
North Pk SL9 41 D5
North Rd,
  Amersham HP6 35 F2
North Rd,
  High Wycombe HP15 16 B1
Northcroft HP10 24 F3
Northdown Rd SL9 40 D1
Northend Rd HP10 24 C3
Northern Heights SL8 25 B5
Northern Woods HP10 24 C3
Nortoft Rd SL9 40 D1
Norwich Ho HP13 16 D6
Norwood Ct HP7 34 C5
Norwood Rd HP10 21 F5
Nugent Ct,
  Chesham HP5 30 C4
Nugent Ct,
  Marlow SL7 27 E5
Nursery Cl,
  Amersham HP6 35 F4
Nursery Cl,
  High Wycombe HP10 17 G6
Nursery Ct HP12 19 E2
Nursery Dr HP14 28 C1
Nursery La HP10 17 G6
Nursery Walk SL7 27 B7
Nutfield La HP11 15 F6
Nutkins Way HP5 30 D6

Oak Cres HP12 18 C4
Oak End Way SL9 41 D7
Oak Rd HP27 4 C5
Oak St HP11 20 A4
Oak Tree Av SL7 27 C5
Oak Tree Cl SL7 27 C5
Oak Tree Dr HP14 28 C2
Oak Tree Rd SL7 26 C4
Oak Vw HP15 12 B3
Oakdene HP9 23 F2

47

Oaken Gro HP16 8 B4
Oakengrove HP13 9 B2
Oakengrove Cl HP15 13 F5
Oakengrove La HP15 17 E2
Oakengrove Rd HP15 17 E2
Oakeshott Av HP14 11 E6
Oakfield HP5 32 B1
Oakfield Cl HP6 34 D2
Oakfield Rd SL8 25 A6
Oakington Av HP6 36 D4
Oakland Way HP10 24 A1
Oaklands Ct HP6 34 D3
Oakley HP10 24 F3
Oakridge Rd HP11 19 E1
Oaktree Cl HP10 17 F4
Oakway HP6 32 C6
Oakwood HP10 20 D6
Octagon Par HP11 3 B4
Ogilvie Rd HP12 15 E6
Old Bells Ct HP5 32 C3
Old Coach Dr HP11 21 E4
Old Farm Cl HP9 28 C6
Old Farm La HP7 35 F6
Old Farm Rd HP13 15 E4
Old Field Cl HP6 36 D4
Old Forge Rd HP10 21 G6
Old Hardenwaye HP13 16 C5
Old Heatherdene Cotts HP15 12 B3
Old Horns La SL7 18 A5
Old Kiln Rd,
  Flackwell Heath HP10 24 B2
Old Kiln Rd,
  Tylers Green HP10 17 F4
Old Lodge Dr HP9 23 F4
Old Moor La HP10 24 F2
Old Papermill Cl HP10 24 F2
Old Shire La WD3 39 H2
Old Station Way HP14 28 C2
Old Town Cl HP9 23 F4
Old Town Farm HP16 9 F2
Old Vicarage Way HP10 25 E6
Old Watery La HP10 24 E2
Oldbury Gro HP9 28 C6
Oldhouse Cl HP11 19 E5
Olivers Paddock SL7 26 C3
One Tree La HP9 23 F2
Onslow Gdns HP13 20 C1
Oram Ct SL7 27 C6
Orbell Ct HP27 4 B4
Orchard Cl,
  Beaconsfield HP9 23 E2
Orchard Cl,
  High Wycombe HP14 11 G5
Orchard Dr,
  Hazlemere HP15 17 E2
Orchard Dr,
  Wooburn HP10 25 D6
Orchard End HP15 13 B6
Orchard End Av HP7 35 G4
Orchard Gro,
  Gerrards Cross SL9 40 B3
Orchard Gro,
  High Wycombe HP10 24 B3
Orchard Ho,
  Bourne End SL8 25 B6
Orchard Ho,
  High Wycombe HP12 18 D4
Orchard La,
  Amersham HP6 35 E3
Orchard La,
  Great Missenden HP16 8 B3
Orchard Leigh Villas HP5 31 H4
Orchard Mews HP9 29 B5
Orchard Mill SL8 25 B8
Orchard Pk HP15 13 G6
Orchard Pl,
  High Wycombe HP14 6 B4
Orchard Pl,
  Princes Risborough HP27 4 C2
Orchard Rd,
  Beaconsfield HP9 23 G4
Orchard Rd,
  Chalfont St Giles HP8 38 D4
Orchard Rd,
  High Wycombe HP13 20 D3
Orchard Rd,
  Seer Green HP9 29 A4
Orchard Way HP15 19 G3
Orchehill Av SL9 41 B6
Orchehill Rise SL9 41 C7

Outfield Rd SL9 40 B3
Outlook Dr HP8 39 E4
Oval Way SL9 41 C6
Over Hampden HP16 8 A2
Over The Misbourne Rd SL9 41 F8
Overdale Rd HP5 30 D5
Overdales HP15 16 D3
Overleigh Ct HP13 3 D2
Overshot Ho HP10 21 F6
Owlsears Cl HP9 23 E1
Oxford Rd,
  Beaconsfield HP9 22 B5
Oxford Rd,
  Gerrards Cross SL9 41 A7
Oxford Rd,
  High Wycombe HP11 3 A3
Oxford Rd,
  Marlow SL7 27 C6
Oxford St,
  Stokenchurch HP14 6 A4
Oxford St,
  Great Missenden HP16 7 C2
Oxford St,
  High Wycombe HP11 3 B4

Packhorse Rd SL9 41 C5
Paddocks End HP9 29 B5
Paget Cl SL7 26 E4
Palliser Rd HP8 38 C5
Pankridge Dr HP16 8 B3
Papermakers Lodge HP11 20 C3
Parade Ct SL8 25 A6
Parchment Cl HP6 35 F2
Parish Piece HP15 13 F5
Park Cl HP14 28 C1
Park Farm Rd HP12 14 C5
Park Farm Way HP14 28 C2
Park Gro HP8 37 C6
Park La,
  Beaconsfield HP9 23 G4
Park La,
  Hazlemere HP15 17 E1
Park La,
  Lane End HP14 28 B2
Park La,
  Stokenchurch HP14 6 B4
Park Lane Ct HP14 6 C4
Park Mdw HP27 4 B5
Park Pl,
  Amersham HP6 35 F3
Park Pl,
  Beaconsfield HP9 29 B4
Park Rd HP6 35 F2
Park St,
  High Wycombe HP11 20 B2
Park St,
  Princes Risborough HP27 4 B4
Parker Knoll Way HP13 3 B3
Parkfield Av HP16 35 E2
Parkhouse Bsns Centre HP12 15 E6
Parkside,
  Gerrards Cross SL9 41 D6
Parkside,
  High Wycombe HP14 10 B3
Parkview HP10 24 B3
Parkview Ct HP12 14 D6
Parkway SL7 26 F4
Parkwood HP14 10 A2
Parliament Cl HP16 8 A2
Parrs Rd HP14 6 C5
Parry Cotts SL9 39 F6
Parsonage Cl HP13 20 A1
Parsonage Gdns SL7 27 D7
Parsonage Pl HP7 34 D4
Parsonage Rd HP8 38 C4
Parsons Walk HP15 13 F6
Partridge Cl HP5 31 F4
Partridge Way HP13 14 C4
Patches Fld SL7 26 D3
Patterson Cl HP10 24 E2
Patterson Rd HP5 30 C5
Pauls Row HP11 3 B4
Pavilion Way HP6 36 C3
Peacock Rd SL7 27 F5
Pear Tree Cl,
  Amersham HP7 35 G4
Pear Tree Cl,
  Beaconsfield HP9 29 A5
Pear Tree Cl HP15 13 G5
Pearce Rd HP5 30 D6
Peatey Ct HP13 20 B2
Peddle Ct HP11 3 A4

Pednor Rd HP5 30 A6
Pednormead End HP5 32 B3
Peel Ct HP27 4 B3
Penfold Cotts HP15 13 H4
Penfold La HP15 13 G4
Penington Rd HP9 22 C5
Penmoor Cl HP12 14 D6
Penn Av HP5 32 B1
Penn Ct,
  High Wycombe HP10 17 F5
Penn Ct, Marlow SL7 27 D6
Penn Gaskell La SL9 39 F6
Penn Grn HP9 23 E2
Penn Rd,
  Beaconsfield HP9 28 B4
Penn Rd,
  Gerrards Cross SL9 40 C3
Penn Rd,
  High Wycombe HP15 17 E2
Pennington Rd,
  Gerrards Cross SL9 40 B2
Pennington Rd,
  High Wycombe HP13 20 D2
Penshurst Cl SL9 40 D1
Pentlands St HP13 21 E4
Penwood La SL7 27 B7
Peppard Mdw HP16 8 A4
Pepys Dr HP16 8 A4
Perch Cl SL7 27 B7
Percy Ter HP8 38 B4
Peregrine Bsns Pk HP13 21 E3
Perks La HP16 11 H1
Perth Rd HP13 16 B5
Peterborough Av HP13 3 D4
Peterley Av HP16 8 D6
Peterley La HP16 12 B1
Peters Cl HP16 8 B3
Peters La HP27 4 D2
Pettifer Way HP12 14 C4
Pheasant Dr HP13 14 C4
Pheasant Hill HP8 38 D4
Pheasant Rise HP5 32 D4
Pheasant Walk SL9 39 H6
Pheasants Dr HP15 13 E6
Pheasants Ridge SL7 26 B1
Phibbs Ho HP16 8 B3
Philip Cotts SL8 25 C6
Philip Dr HP10 24 C3
Philip Rd HP13 20 B1
Philps Ct HP14 28 C2
Phoenix Bsns Centre HP5 32 C1
Phoenix Point HP18 18 D3
Picts La HP27 4 A6
Pigeon Farm Rd HP14 6 C4
Piggotts End HP7 34 C5
Piggotts Hill HP14 11 E1
Piggotts Orch HP14 34 C5
Pike Cl SL7 27 B7
Pilgrims Cl HP27 4 B2
Pilot Trading Est HP12 15 E6
Pimms Cl HP13 21 E2
Pimms Gro HP13 21 E2
Pine Chase HP12 18 C4
Pine Cl HP15 17 E3
Pine Hill HP15 16 D3
Pine Walk HP15 17 E3
Pineapple Rd HP7 35 G4
Pinecroft SL7 27 C5
Pinels Way HP11 19 E5
Pines Cl,
  Amersham HP6 34 C1
Pines Cl,
  Great Missenden HP16 9 G5
Pinetree Cl SL9 40 A3
Pinewood Rd HP12 14 C6
Pinions Rd HP13 20 B3
Pink Rd HP27 5 A2
Pipers La HP15 12 A4
Pitch Pond Cl HP9 28 B6
Place Farm Ho HP27 4 B2
Place Farm Mews HP27 4 B2
Place Farm Way HP27 4 B2
Plantation Rd,
  Amersham HP6 35 E2
Plantation Rd, High Wycombe HP13 21 E1
Plantation Way HP6 35 F2
Plomer Green Av HP13 14 D4
Plomer Green La HP13 14 D2
Plomer Hill HP13 14 D5
Plumer Rd HP12 19 E1
Poles Hill HP5 30 B6

Polidoris La HP15 13 G5
Pomeroy Cl HP7 35 E5
Pond App HP15 13 G5
Pond Cotts,
  High Wycombe HP14 28 C3
Pond Cotts,
  Princes Risborough HP27 5 C3
Pond Field Cotts HP6 29 B2
Pond La SL9 40 A4
Pond Park Rd HP5 30 C6
Pondwicks HP7 34 B5
Popes Cl HP6 35 F2
Poplar Av HP7 35 G4
Poplar Cl HP5 30 D4
Poplar Rd HP10 24 E2
Poppy Rd HP27 4 A5
Portland Gdns SL7 27 C7
Portland Ho HP13 16 B6
Portland Pk SL9 41 C8
Portlands Alley SL7 27 C7
Portobello Cl HP5 30 C6
Portobello Cotts HP27 5 B3
Portway Dr HP12 14 B4
Post Office La HP9 23 E2
Potter Row HP16 7 A4
Potters Cl HP16 8 A2
Potters Cross Cres HP15 16 C4
Potts Pl SL7 27 C6
Pound Cres SL7 27 C7
Pound La SL7 27 B8
Pratt Ho HP6 35 G3
Preston Hill HP5 31 E5
Prestwood Cl HP12 14 D6
Pretoria Rd HP13 16 A6
Priestley Ct HP13 20 B2
Priests Paddock HP9 28 B6
Primrose Cotts HP14 11 E2
Primrose Grn HP13 12 D5
Primrose Hill HP15 12 D4
Primrose Lea SL7 27 C6
Princes Cl SL8 25 C6
Princes Gate HP13 20 B2
Princes La HP16 7 C2
Princes Rd SL8 25 C6
Prior Gro HP5 32 D1
Priory Av HP13 3 B3
Priory Rd,
  Gerrards Cross SL9 41 B5
Priory Rd,
  High Wycombe HP13 3 B4
Priory Way SL9 41 B5
Progress Rd HP12 18 B1
Prospect Cotts,
  Amersham HP7 35 G4
Prospect Cotts,
  Bourne End SL8 25 D7
Prospect Cotts,
  High Wycombe HP14 10 D6
Prospect Ct HP14 28 B2
Prospect Rd SL7 27 C5
Prospect Works HP5 32 C3
Puers La HP9 29 C5
Pulfields HP5 32 B1
Pulpit Cl HP5 30 B6
Pump La HP5 33 E5
Pump La North SL9 26 E2
Pump La South SL7 26 F3
Pump Mdw HP16 9 F2
Punch Bowl La HP5 32 C3
Pursell Pl HP27 4 B3
Pursells Mdw HP14 10 D5
Pusey Way HP14 28 C1
Pyebush La HP9 23 H6
Pymcombe Cl HP27 4 B3
Pyramid Ho HP11 3 A3

Quarrendon Rd HP7 35 E5
Quarry Wood Rd SL7 27 D7
Quarrydale Dr SL7 26 E6
Quebec Rd HP13 20 C2
Queen Alexandra Rd HP11 3 A5
Queen Sq HP11 3 B4
Queen St HP13 20 A1
Queen Victoria Rd HP11 3 C5
Queens Acre HP13 20 A2
Queens Cl HP13 20 A2
Queens Rd,
  Chesham HP5 32 C1
Queens Rd,
  High Wycombe HP13 20 A2
Queens Rd,
  Marlow SL7 27 C6

Queens,
  Princes Risborough HP27
Queens Sq HP27
Queensmead Ho HP10
Queensmead Rd HP10
Queensway HP15
Quickberry Pl HP7
Quill Hall La HP6
Quoiting Sq SL7
Quoitings Dr SL7
Quoitings Gdns SL7

Raans Rd HP6
Rachels Way HP5
Raeside Cl HP9
Ragmans Cl SL7
Ragmans La SL7
Ragstones HP10
Ralphs Retreat HP15
Ramsay Vw HP15
Ramscote La HP5
Raven Rd HP14
Ravenshoe Cl HP13
Ravensmead SL9
Raylands Mead SL9
Raylens HP12
Rayners Av HP10
Rayners Cl HP10
Rays La HP10
Rays Yd HP10
Ream Ct HP11
Recreation Rd SL8
Rectory Av HP13
Rectory Ct,
  Amersham HP7
Rectory Ct,
  High Wycombe HP13
Rectory Gdns HP8
Rectory Hill HP7
Rectory Way HP7
Red House Cl HP9
Red Lion Dr HP14
Red Lion St HP5
Red Lion Way HP10
Redding Dr HP6
Redgrave Pl SL7
Redhouse Cl HP11
Redhouse Farm Cotts HP27
Redman Ct HP27
Redman Rd HP12
Redshots Cl SL7
Redwood Cl HP15
Redwood Pl HP9
Regius Ct HP10
Rennie Cl HP13
Repton Rd HP7
Revel Rd HP10
Reyners Grn HP16
Reynolds Cl HP13
Reynolds Rd HP9
Reynolds Walk HP5
Richard Gdns HP13
Richmond Cl HP6
Richmond Ct HP13
Rickmansworth La SL9
Rickmansworth Rd HP6
Ridge Cl HP14
Ridge Side HP14
Ridge Way HP13
Ridgemount End SL9
Ridgeway HP11
Ridgeway Cl,
  Chesham HP5
Ridgeway Cl,
  Marlow SL7
Ridgeway Rd HP5
Riding La HP9
Ridings Cotts HP15
Rignall Rd HP16
Riley Rd SL7
Ring Rd HP10
Ripley Cl HP13
River Vw HP10
Riverholme SL8
Riverlock Ct HP11
Rivermead Ct SL8
Riverpark Dr SL7
Rivers Edge HP11
Riversdale SL7
Riversdale Cotts SL8
Riversdale Ct SL8
Riversdale Ho SL8
Riverside SL7

Suffield Rd HP11 3 A5
Summerleys Rd HP27 4 A4
Sunningdale Cl HP12 18 B3
Sunny Bank HP15 12 D5
Sunny Cft HP13 14 C4
Sunnybank SL7 26 C4
Sunnymede Av HP5 31 F4
Sunnyside Cotts HP5 31 H2
Sunnyside Rd HP5 32 C1
Sunters End HP12 18 B1
Sunters Wood Cl HP12 18 C3
Sussex Cl,
 Chalfont St Giles HP8 38 C4
Sussex Cl,
 High Wycombe HP13 16 B5
Swains La HP10 24 B1
Swains Market HP10 24 B1
Swallow Dr HP15 17 E1
Swan Cl HP5 30 C4
Sycamore Cl,
 Amersham HP6 34 D2
Sycamore Cl,
 Bourne End SL8 25 C6
Sycamore Cl,
 Chalfont St Giles HP8 38 B4
Sycamore Corner HP6 34 D2
Sycamore Dene HP5 31 F5
Sycamore Dr SL7 26 C3
Sycamore Ho,
 Amersham HP6 34 D2
Sycamore Ho,
 Princes Risborough
 HP27 4 B4
Sycamore Pl HP6 34 D3
Sycamore Rd,
 Amersham HP6 34 D2
Sycamore Rd,
 Chalfont St Giles HP8 38 B4
Sycamore Rd,
 High Wycombe HP12 18 C4
Sycamore Rise HP8 38 B4
Sycamore Way HP15 17 E2
Sylvia Cl HP16 9 G5

Tadros Ct HP13 20 B2
Talbot Av HP13 14 D4
Tall Oaks HP6 35 E2
Tamar Cl HP13 21 F4
Tancred Rd HP13 15 G5
Tannery Rd HP13 21 E4
Tanton Ho HP16 9 E2
Taplin Way HP10 17 F5
Tapping Rd HP14 28 C2
Tate Rd SL9 39 G6
Tavistock Mews HP12 15 E6
Taylors Cl SL7 27 E6
Taylors Rd HP5 31 E6
Taylors Turn HP13 14 D3
Teal Ho HP11 20 A2
Technology Ho SL8 25 C6
Telford Way HP13 3 A1
Telston Cl SL8 24 B4
Templars Pl SL7 27 D7
Temple End HP13 3 B3
Temple Gate HP13 3 B3
Temple Ho SL8 25 B6
Temple Orch HP13 3 D3
Temple St HP11 3 A4
Tennyson Rd HP11 19 G3
Tenterden HP6 33 E6
Tenzing Dr HP13 20 C2
Terrington Hill SL7 27 B6
Terry Orch HP13 16 A6
Terry Rd HP13 16 A6
Terryfield Rd HP13 20 B2
Tetherdown HP16 8 B5
Thame Ho HP13 3 C4
Thames Cl SL8 25 A6
Thames Ind Est SL7 27 E6
Thamesfield Gdns
 SL7 27 D7
Thanestead Copse
 HP10 21 G6
Thanestead Ct HP10 21 G6
The Acre SL7 27 F5
The Acres HP13 15 E5
The Arcade,
 Beaconsfield HP9 23 F3
The Arcade,
 High Wycombe HP11 3 B4
The Avenue,
 Amersham HP7 34 D3
The Avenue,
 Bourne End SL8 25 A5
The Avenue,
 Princes Risborough
 HP27 4 C3

The Backs HP5 32 C2
The Beeches HP6 34 B1
The Birches HP13 16 B6
The Brackens HP11 20 A3
The Braid HP5 31 F6
The Briars,
 High Wycombe HP11 20 A3
The Briars,
 Holmer Green HP15 13 G5
The Broadway HP7 34 C5
The Brow HP8 39 E4
The Bsns Centre HP6 35 G3
The Burren HP6 34 D2
The Bury Farm HP5 32 B3
The Causeway SL7 27 D7
The Chalfonts &
 Gerrards Cross Hospital
 SL9 40 B3
The Chalkpits HP10 24 E4
The Chase,
 Chesham HP5 30 D6
The Chase,
 High Wycombe HP10 17 F4
The Chase,
 Marlow SL7 27 F5
The Cherry Pit HP13 15 E3
The Chiltern Hospital
 HP16 9 G5
The Chilterns Shop Centre
 HP11 3 B4
The Chimes HP12 19 F2
The Chyne SL9 41 D7
The Cloisters HP13 16 B4
The Close,
 Bourne End SL8 26 A4
The Close,
 Marlow SL7 27 A6
The Common,
 Flackwell Heath HP10 24 B1
The Common,
 Great Kingshill HP15 12 B3
The Common,
 Holmer Green HP15 13 G4
The Coppice,
 Beaconsfield HP9 29 B5
The Coppice,
 Booker HP12 18 C4
The Coppice,
 Great Kingshill HP15 12 C3
The Coppice,
 Walters Ash HP14 10 C4
The Copse,
 Amersham HP7 34 D3
The Copse,
 Beaconsfield HP9 22 D1
The Courtyard,
 Bourne End SL8 25 B6
The Courtyard,
 High Wycombe HP10 24 E2
The Courtyard,
 Marlow SL7 27 D6
The Crescent,
 High Wycombe HP13 16 C6
The Crescent,
 Princes Risborough
 HP27 4 C4
The Crest,
 Beaconsfield HP9 22 C4
The Crest,
 High Wycombe HP14 6 A3
The Croft SL7 27 F5
The Dell,
 Gerrards Cross SL9 40 D1
The Dell,
 Stokenchurch HP14 6 D6
The Dell,
 Tylers Green HP10 17 F5
The Drey SL9 40 C1
The Drive,
 Amersham HP7 34 D3
The Drive,
 Bourne End SL8 25 A6
The Drive,
 Gerrards Cross SL9 40 D3
The Fairway HP10 24 C2
The Farthings HP6 35 E1
The Fennings HP14 34 D1
The Ferns HP9 23 G5
The Garth HP16 9 F2
The Gateway Centre
 HP12 18 D3
The Glade HP10 17 F4
The Glebe,
 Great Missenden HP168 A3
The Glebe,
 High Wycombe HP14 11 E5
The Gowers HP6 35 E1

The Green,
 Amersham HP7 34 D3
The Green,
 Chalfont St Giles
 HP8 38 D4
The Green,
 High Wycombe HP10 24 F4
The Green Acres HP13 16 A4
The Greenway,
 Gerrards Cross SL9 41 C5
The Greenway,
 High Wycombe HP13 3 C4
The Greenway,
 Tylers Green HP10 17 F4
The Grove,
 Amersham HP6 33 E6
The Grove,
 Chesham HP5 36 C1
The Hawthorns,
 Chalfont St Giles HP8 37 B5
The Hawthorns,
 Flackwell Heath HP10 24 B2
The Hawthorns,
 High Wycombe HP14 28 B2
The Hawthorns,
 Princes Risborough
 HP27 4 C1
The Hawthorns,
 Woburn Green HP10 24 F4
The Haystacks HP13 3 C4
The Hollies HP9 23 F2
The Holloway HP27 4 D2
The Homestead,
 Booker HP12 18 D5
The Homestead,
 Great Kingshill HP15 12 A2
The Lagger HP8 38 C4
The Larches,
 Amersham HP6 36 B3
The Larches,
 High Wycombe HP15 13 G5
The Larchlands HP10 17 G4
The Laurels HP12 18 C4
The Lawns HP10 17 F4
The Leys HP6 32 C6
The Limes HP6 32 C6
The Lincolns HP16 13 E1
The Link HP15 13 E6
The Maltings HP7 34 B4
The Mead HP9 23 G3
The Meadows,
 Amersham HP7 35 E4
The Meadows,
 High Wycombe HP10 24 B1
The Mercury Pk HP10 24 F3
The Merlin Centre
 HP12 19 E3
The Middleway HP13 3 C4
The Millstream HP11 20 A2
The Octagon Shop Centre
 HP11 3 B4
The Old Garden Centre
 HP27 4 B4
The Orchard,
 Flackwell Heath HP10 24 C3
The Orchard,
 Marlow SL7 27 D5
The Orchard,
 Naphill HP14 11 E6
The Orchard,
 Widmer End HP15 13 E6
The Orchards HP13 13 E1
The Paddock SL9 40 C1
The Paddocks,
 Booker HP12 18 B5
The Paddocks,
 Flackwell Heath HP10 24 B2
The Paddocks,
 Great Missenden HP168 B6
The Paddocks Hospital
 HP27 4 C3
The Parade,
 Bourne End SL8 25 B6
The Parade,
 High Wycombe HP11 19 F2
The Park Par Centre
 HP15 17 E1
The Pastures HP13 15 E4
The Penningtons HP13 35 E2
The Pentlands HP13 21 E4
The Phygtle SL9 40 D1
The Pines HP10 17 F5
The Platt HP7 34 B5
The Quadrangle HP13 20 C1
The Quadrant HP13 16 C6
The Queensway SL9 41 C5

The Retreat,
 Amersham HP6 36 E4
The Retreat,
 Princes Risborough
 HP27 4 B4
The Ridgeway,
 Amersham HP7 35 E5
The Ridgeway,
 Gerrards Cross SL9 41 C5
The Ridgeway,
 Marlow SL7 26 D4
The Ridings,
 Amersham HP6 33 E6
The Ridings,
 Chesham HP5 36 D1
The Rise,
 Amersham HP7 34 D4
The Rise,
 Loudwater HP13 21 F4
The Rise,
 Widmer End HP15 13 E6
The Risings HP13 15 H5
The Roperies HP13 20 C2
The Rosary HP15 13 F5
The Rosary SL8 25 A6
The Row HP14 28 B2
The Rowans SL9 41 B5
The Rushes SL7 27 B7
The Russets SL9 40 B4
The Sidings HP11 21 E5
The Spinney,
 Beaconsfield HP9 23 E5
The Spinney,
 Chesham HP5 31 F6
The Spinney,
 High Wycombe HP11 19 G4
The Spinney,
 Holmer Green HP15 13 H5
The Square HP16 9 G3
The Thicket HP15 17 E5
The Vale SL9 40 C3
The Valley Centre
 HP13 20 A1
The Warren,
 Chesham HP5 30 A5
The Warren,
 Gerrards Cross SL9 40 E3
The Warren,
 High Wycombe HP15 12 D6
The Water Gdns HP15 16 C4
The Waterglades HP9 28 C5
The Willows HP6 32 B6
The Woodlands,
 Amersham HP6 32 D6
The Woodlands,
 High Wycombe HP10 16 D3
The Worthies HP7 34 B5
Third Av SL7 27 F6
Third St HP11 19 H4
Thomas Rd HP10 25 D5
Thornaby Pl HP10 24 F2
Thorne Rd HP14 28 C2
Thornhill Cl HP7 34 B5
Three Gables HP9 23 F3
Three Holds HP8 38 A5
Thrush Cl HP12 18 C3
Tierney Ct SL7 27 D7
Tilbury Wood Cl HP13 14 C4
Tilecotes Cl SL7 27 C6
Tilling Cres HP13 20 D1
Tilsworth Rd HP9 22 D5
Tinkers Wood Rd
 HP13 15 E4
Tipping Way HP14 6 C4
Todd Cl HP15 13 F5
Tom Evans Ct HP13 3 C1
Toms Turn HP15 16 D1
Tooks Ct HP12 19 E3
Top Farm Cft HP9 22 B4
Top Pk SL9 41 B8
Topland Rd SL9 40 B3
Totteridge Av HP13 20 A1
Totteridge Dr HP13 16 B5
Totteridge La HP13 16 B4
Totteridge Par HP13 16 B5
Totteridge Rd HP13 3 C4
Tower Cl HP10 24 D3
Tower Ct HP27 4 B4
Tower Ho SL7 27 A7
Tower Rd HP13 16 B4
Toweridge La HP12 14 A6
Towers Lea HP13 3 D4
Town Bridge Ct HP5 32 C3
Town Field La HP8 38 D4
Town La HP10 25 D6
Town Lane Cotts HP10 25 E5
Townfield HP5 32 C2

Townfield Rd HP13
Townsend Rd HP5
Townsends Reach SL8
Trafford Cl HP16
Trafford Rd HP16
Trapps Ct HP5
Trapps La HP5
Treachers Cl HP5
Treadaway Bsns Centre
 HP10
Treadaway Hill HP10
Treadaway Rd HP10
Trees Av HP14
Trees Rd,
 Bourne End SL8
Trees Rd,
 High Wycombe HP14
Trinity Av SL7
Trinity Ct,
 Chesham HP5
Trinity Ct, Marlow SL7
Trinity Rd,
 High Wycombe HP15
Trinity Rd,
 Marlow SL7
Tripps Hill Cl HP8
Trout Cl SL7
Tucker Ct HP13
Tuckers Dr HP15
Tudor Ct,
 Amersham HP6
Tudor Ct,
 Gerrards Cross SL9
Tudor Dr HP10
Tudor Pk HP6
Tudor Rd HP15
Tulkers Cl HP16
Tunmers Ct SL9
Tunmers End SL9
Turners Dr HP13
Turners Fld HP13
Turners Pl HP15
Turners Walk HP5
Turners Wood Dr HP8
Turnpike Rd HP12
Turnpike Way HP12
Tweenways HP5
Twitchell Rd HP16
Twitchells La HP9
Two Dells La HP5
Twyford Pl HP12
Tylers Cres HP15
Tylers Hill Rd HP5
Tylers Rd HP15
Tylsworth Cl HP6
Tyzack Rd HP13

Ufton Ct SL8
Underwood Rd HP13
Union Ind Est HP12
Union St HP11
Up Corner HP8
Up Corner Cl HP8
Upland Av HP5
Uplands SL7
Uplands Cl HP14
Uplands Ct HP5
Upper Belmont Rd
 HP5
Upper Dr HP9
Upper George St HP5
Upper Green St HP11
Upper Hollis HP16
Upper Hughenden Rd
 HP14
Upper Icknield Way,
 Princes Risborough
 HP27
Upper Icknield Way,
 Whiteleaf HP27
Upper Lodge La HP15
Upper Riding HP9
Upway SL9

Vache La HP8
Vache Mews HP8
Vale Cl SL9
Vale Rd HP5
Vale Rise HP5
Valentine Way HP8
Valley Rd HP14
Valley Vw HP5
Valley Way SL9
Vanguard Cl HP12
Verney Av HP12
Verney Cl SL7
Vicarage Cl HP9